Thomas Sheridan, Saxe Bannister

Some Revelations in Irish History

or, old elements of creed and class conciliation

Thomas Sheridan, Saxe Bannister

Some Revelations in Irish History
or, old elements of creed and class conciliation

ISBN/EAN: 9783744717311

Printed in Europe, USA, Canada, Australia, Japan

Cover: Foto ©ninafisch / pixelio.de

More available books at **www.hansebooks.com**

SOME

REVELATIONS IN IRISH HISTORY;

OR, OLD ELEMENTS OF

CREED AND CLASS CONCILIATION

IN IRELAND.

EDITED BY SAXE BANNISTER, M.A.,

OF LINCOLN'S INN, FORMERLY ATTORNEY-GENERAL
IN NEW SOUTH WALES.

LONDON:

LONGMANS, GREEN, READER, AND DYER.

1870.

THIS LITTLE VOLUME IS INSCRIBED TO THE

MEMORY OF

DR. WILLIAM BEDELL,

OF ESSEX, SOME TIME FELLOW OF EMANUEL COLLEGE,
CAMBRIDGE ; MANY YEARS CHAPLAIN
TO THE BRITISH EMBASSY
IN VENICE ;
PROVOST OF TRINITY COLLEGE, DUBLIN, AND
LORD BISHOP OF KILMORE
AND ARDAGH.

IN Italy, during a defigned feceffion from the Romifh Church, this worthy Proteftant prelate gained the confidence of the leaders in that critical movement towards religious reform.

In Ireland, during longer and harder trials, he enjoyed the univerfal refpect due to his pre-eminent qualities.

To other vaft intellectual acquirements he added familiarity with the ancient language of the Irifh people, fo as to be venerated by the lowlieft among them. In the awful Rebellion of 1641, when he died at an advanced age, his remains were followed to the tomb by "wild Kerns," eager to do honour to his memory.

By a life of piety, toleration, and good works, BISHOP BEDELL had even calmed fome of the terrors of a fearful time.

His admirable example, then, and his marvellous fuccefs may well encourage us in our tafk of ftaying dangers only lefs fearful, by a rule of juftice in the fame troubled land.

THE EDITOR'S PREFACE.

I. In Ireland, during all ages, elements have exifted for uniting all its people, of every origin, and every creed. The ancient fact on that head confirmed by the recent experience of Thomas Drummond. Illuftrations of the fact in the laft two centuries,—the cafe of the Ulfter Settlements by citizens of London; and the prodigious moral power of Dr. Bedell of Effex, Lord Bifhop of Kilmore, from 1629 to the Rebellion of 1641. II. The Anglo-Irifh family of the Sheridans of the 17th century—fruits of both influences. III. The Tract of 1677 and 1685, on Parliamentary and all focial reforms, by Thomas Sheridan, a member of that family. IV. Thomas Sheridan, Secretary to the Government and a Privy Councillor in Ireland, 1687. His exile in France; and his hiftory of the reign of James II., a MS. preferved in the Royal Library at Windfor. The Stuart MSS. at home and abroad.

I.

THE hiftory of Ireland is fhown in the few contents of this little volume, not to be wanting in evidence favourable to the advent of a peaceful and profperous union of that ifland of Celts, or by whatever name its mixed inhabitants of many origins are to be known, with the people of Great Britain, compofed of no lefs diverfe races. Hitherto, indeed, fuch union, although earneftly fought by the wifeft, has been utterly unattainable in confequence of the deep-feated vicious defire of territorial conquefts prevailing over the better fenfe of conftitutional duty, fignified by the folemn declaration in an Act of Parliament, that, " to make wars for conqueft's fake is repugnant to the wifhes and genius of the Britifh people."[1] That welcome evidence will, however, be accepted without reluctance. Yet, notwithftanding its force, good writers continue to hold to this day, and they are fupported by a common belief, that fome myfterious adverfe temperaments naturally divide our refpective populations, fixing them eternally in " hoftile camps." Long ago, on the other hand, in a like controverfy, it was maintained fagacioufly, that ftriking difcrepancies in the focial conditions of different nations, have a more intelligible fource in the character of governments, not in climate or parentage. Surely, moreover, even the few authentic facts here produced muft, although much neglected by ftatefmen, tend triumphantly to filence the wretched ftrife fo long ruinous to Ireland,

[1] 1784, 24 Geo. III. c. 25, fect. 34; and 1793, 33 Geo. III. c. 52, fect. 42.

nor lefs coftly to Great Britain. Nor is any thing here offered for confideration, effentially inconfiftent with the vaft hiftorical ftores now at length opening among us officially in order to clear up all paft obfcurities in the national annals. The fpeculative profpect too, of a hopeful iffue in our onward career, is wonderfully ftrengthened by the teftimony of the very ableft adminiftrator ever engaged in the holy miffion of popular conciliation in Ireland. This was the late Thomas Drummond, who won the hearts of the whole Irifh people. He it was who declared, with fatal truth, that, to our mutual damage, Ireland is ftill unknown to the Britifh people.[1] He did better. By familiar ftudy of the Irifh popular character from his early manhood to the clofe of his too fhort career, he learned to know it well. Then he as bravely fpoke out what he knew to the credit of the people, fo as to obtain large affent to his intelligent defigns for the benefit of the hard-tried land. His elaborate teftimony before a Parliamentary Committee—the Roden Committee of 1839; his famous maxim, that "property has its duties as well as its rights;"[2] and his official meafures,

---

[1] M'Lennan's Life of Thomas Drummond, Edinburgh, 8vo., 1867, p. 354.   [2] Ibid. p. 322.

might be cited with confidence on this head. But all this was simply the fruit of his keen insight into the trustworthiness of the peasantry as he met them in their wild mountains during the Irish survey so long ago as in 1823. "I am sure," he said, in effect, "that all fear of mischief to our work from these Irish is unfounded. They will not damage a man exposed on the hills."[1] His wife conclusion was, that Ireland needs only justice for her regeneration, and that with just measures vigorously carried out, our union will never be broken.

His personal experiences alone seem to have led this eminent statesman of our day, to act upon a strong confidence in native Irish capabilities, unaware as he may have been of genial convictions like his own having in less auspicious times induced others as worthy as himself, to struggle for better rule in Ireland only to be disappointed. The object of this volume is to reproduce a good work of one of the most memorable of those older worthies exactly as he originally wrote it, with a brief sketch of some of the happier antecedents, and probably the seeds of his labours.

The recently published able record of Thomas Drummond's great success when relying on the

---

[1] M'Lennan's Life of Thomas Drummond, p. 111.

better fide of Irifh popular life, is fingularly opportune, imperfect as its contents unavoidably are.[1]

This frank ftatement of the year 1867 will certainly be expunged from an enlarged edition of this book, to be called for under the more promifing Irifh influence of 1870. We have reached the dawn of brighter things than thofe which were accomplifhed fo well by the laft generation with their lights; and the whole truth concerning the paft can now be told with advantage on all fides. For this end, all of the paft that ought to have been general, muft be held up to honour now. Its record is richer and richer every day. In the laft century much in that way was well begun. The great Houfe of Ormond was then fet forth in brilliant colours; although its earlier ftory was by no means exhaufted. The *Houfe of Ivery* too, did juftice to the good Percevals of Ireland. In the *Hibernica* valuable documents from the Conqueft downward, were fet forth by Walter Harris. In the *Anthologia*, publifhed in Dublin in 1793, young Colonel Arthur Wellefley, ever ready in his place

---

[1] "Drummond's political correfpondence during his tenure of office in Ireland, carried on with fome of the moft important political perfonages of the time, I have not had at my difpofal."— *Preface to M'Lennan's Memoir of Thomas Drummond.*

for the duties of civil life, ranked himſelf freely with the foremoſt of the enlightened heads[1] and hopes[2] of popular Ireland, to inſtruct and encourage her people. The times are improving upon even thoſe. The ſplendid work upon the Iriſh *Forteſcues* in their juſt connection with a kindred Engliſh worthy, is every way a moſt important contribution to our united hiſtory; whilſt already in the firſt report of the Royal Commiſſion on our Hiſtorical MSS., we have official notice of the invaluable Charlemont papers on the laſt century's Iriſh events, and eſpecially of others of equal intereſt poſſeſſed by the Lord Talbot de Malahide reſpecting the revolution of 1688. In both will be found genuine materials to correct grave errors in the pages of our beſt hiſtorians.

Age after age exhibits diſtinctly the better Iriſh tendencies, but only to be thwarted by the monſtrous rule of conqueſt,—a vulgar repetition of brute " force,"—the βίη of the ancients, rejected by the very Pagan philoſophers as an unworthy principle of government. Two comparatively modern ex-

---

[1] *e. g.* Dr. Troy and Theobald Wolfe Tone, found among the ſubſcribers to this Anthologia.

[2] " Maſter Thomas Moore, of Trinity College," and " Miſs Owenſon " are among firſt ſubſcribers.

amples of wifer policy here offered from the annals of Ireland eftablifh beyond difpute, the great truth, that even the leaft refined of her people eftimate correctly the benefit of juft relations with their fellow men.

The Ulfter Settlements by citizens of London.

The firft example belongs to the reign of James I. It is the cafe of the fettlements in Ulfter managed by citizens of London. In that reign a partial paufe occurred in the deadly conflicts between the native Irifh and their conquerors. In Ulfter new fettlements, Englifh and Scottifh, were formed upon conditions, partaking, indeed, too much of the fpirit of hoftility to the natives, but at the fame time with material tendencies to peaceable union; fo that the advice of Sir John Davies on the occafion, to crufh the Irifh by the fword, was not literally adopted by King James in a project aiming at mixed tenancies. Exprefs provifion was made in that project for grants to the new colonifts—to the civil and military fervants of the crown—and alfo to fome Irifh freeholders and leafeholders, who were to occupy the lower lands of Ulfter—not the more defenfible hills. The " Sword-men " only among the Irifh were to be difperfed in new homes in a remote province.[1] The City of London adopted warmly the part of the enterprife which gave large tracts of land in the north for fettlements. The original memorial fubmitted by the citizens to the king indicates the noble character of their views by an extremely interefting recital. At the conqueft of Ireland by Henry II. they fay, when Dublin, a ruin under the ravages of the Efterlings, was granted to the citizens of Briftol, one object of the colonifts of that early time was to "civilize" the native Irifh; and the citizens of London now accepted the cited precedent for their own guidance. Indeed, this official ufe in the feventeenth century of the fingle word "civilize" to characterife a work of five hundred years before, fpeaks volumes for the intention being deliberately formed by the new colonifts, to follow the good example fet by our people of old. Nor is it without fignificance to find this ftate paper with its key-word confpicuous, in a collection of documents juft reftored to us by the North-American government, and depofited with due acknowledgment in our Public Record Office. It conftitutes a grave adminiftrative document of more than hiftorical value, and it is come opportunely, not only in relation to

[1] *Hibernica*, by Walter Harris. Dublin, 1770, pp. 237-243.

Ireland, but throughout our whole empire beyond sea, where our duty to "civilize" millions of less advanced men has been forgotten these thirty years.

The civilization thus promised by Bristol, as an advantage to the Irish, had its various elements; and at the earlier period of the conquest, marriage was not uncommon, even between the noblest of the invaders and the daughters of the native chiefs, whilst these chiefs often fought to form free and integral political union with the English. At length in that earlier period, the less conciliatory rule prevailed; and in 1367, the Statutes of Kilkenny prohibited such marriages, which had become frequent. This was done in the identical evil spirit which led the French colonial slave-owners, in the last century, to make the marriages of negroes with white women, capital offences. In both cases, the spirit of assumed superiority was struggling against natural instinct and wise policy. From that time is to be dated the decline of English power in Ireland during one hundred and fifty years; and then under the Tudors for another century, wars were carried on to set up a new tyranny, not less costly to England than hateful to the Irish people. Never was domination bought so dear.

Preface.

Among the undertakers of the more promiſing plantation of James I. in the north of Ireland, the citizens of London were conſpicuous; and they ſucceeded by liberally taking Iriſh among their tenants. So proſperous was this practice that a fierce oppoſition to it was got up by ſome who would willingly cruſh thoſe natives. The name of the leader in that oppoſition has come down to us; and the incident merits larger expoſure than can be given in theſe pages. His own ſtatement of the caſe ſufficiently confutes it. " The citizens of London," he ſays, " finding the natives willing to overgive rather than remove, and half the profit only could be got from the Britiſh, whilſt the Iriſh would pay and be uſed at the Londoners' pleaſure, took them as tenants," thus laying the Engliſh open to be ſurpriſed and maſſacred.[1]

But according to documents of later date in the Public Record Office, this ill-will had its proper puniſhment.

In 1630 the Secretary of State writes: " For the great buſineſs of the plantations of the Londoners, Sir Thomas Philips has ſent me ſuch a heap of papers. They are well worth the labour. The

[1] *Hibernica*, Letter of Sir Thomas Philips to the King, p. 247.

Londoners are powerful."[1] Afterwards the Secretary writes:—"I have met Sir Thomas Philips. It grieves me to fee him fo much dejected, having fpent all he had, doing the king good fervice; but difrefpected. Speedy comfort is moft urgent to him."[2]

The ftruggle againft the Londoners in Ulfter, indicated in thefe few lines, lafted a whole generation, until they were juftified; and their ultimate management of their lands is believed to be excellent, contributing, perhaps, to the good underftanding between the wealthier people in this province and the occupiers of the land, under the fomewhat obfcure term of Ulfter-right. Few books would be more ufeful than a narrative from the abundant fources extant, of the Londoners' fettlement in Ireland the laft 250 years, with its bearing on that famous right.

Dr. Bedell, Lord Bifhop of Kilmore.

This Englifh divine, born in Effex in 1570, and a fellow of Emanuel College, Cambridge, was for eight years chaplain to our embaffy in Venice.

---

[1] Public Record Office, Domeftic, Charles I., vol. clxxii. No. 72, p. 330.

[2] Ibid. vol. clxxv. No. 121.

Preface.

There he was distinguished for the deepest learning, by his aptitude for modern languages no less than for classical and Biblical attainments. He spoke Italian so fluently that great scholars in Italy eagerly sought his converse, and the time of his residence there being that of a contemplated separation of Venice from the Church of Rome, his familiar relations with ecclesiastics and others of the highest repute, tended much to promote the expected schism. In 1626 he was appointed by King Charles I. provost of Trinity College, Dublin, in order to reform some disorders there. In 1628, at the mature age of fifty-eight, he was made Bishop of Kilmore. This see he held until his decease, thirteen years later, in the height of the Irish rebellion of 1641. The exemplary discharge of all the duties of his diocese gained him the affectionate veneration of the wildest people at a moment of sanguinary uprising unexampled even in Ireland.

At his death, so great was the alarm of crowds of English victims sheltered under his roof, that they durst not attend his body to the grave. The rebels however took that duty upon themselves. " He is the last Englishman," they said, " to be a Bishop here. Nevertheless he was our friend, our father. No honour at our hands can enough prove the love we bore him." A Roman Catholic prieſt who had often been the prelate's gueſt, took part in the burial ceremony, and declared at the brink of the grave that he fervently truſted his own ſpirit would be permitted to meet Biſhop Bedell's bleſſed ſpirit in the better world. Even the Romiſh prelate who was to occupy the ſee of Kilmore after his expulſion, beſought him earneſtly to ſtay and be his gueſt in the epiſcopal palace.

This really marvellous triumph in a ſeaſon of awful diſaſter, muſt be attributable, ſays his biographer, Biſhop Burnet, to miraculous agency; but the narrative carefully written from the mouths of eye-witneſſes, leaves no doubt reſpecting its natural cauſes. Dr. Bedell after his great exemplar, lived a life of doing good. His lordſhip rapidly learned the Iriſh language ſo as to uſe it not only in his church ſervices, but in his daily intercourſe with the people. He alſo tranſlated into Iriſh, religious tracts for popular reading. He even procured the Bible to be tranſlated; and at his death he was prepared to publiſh that tranſlation at his own coſt. Three years later, what he had prepared was publiſhed by the care of Robert Boyle.

By his own example in reſigning his additional ſee of Ardagh, and by his ſtrict diſcipline, his lordship put a stop to the great scandal of plurality in his diocese, and enforced residence. Converts to Protestantism from among the priests were frequent under his ministry; and he carefully provided them with livings. His hospitality was unbounded, and the meanest Irish found him their adviser, entertainer, and friend. At the same time his intercourse with the highest officials was dignified and independent—his care to avoid excesses in the ecclesiastical courts, was unsparing.

Above all, Bishop Bedell enforced the duty of concord with all whose religious opinions he most disliked, as shown in a sermon preached soon after some heats in the House of Commons in the Parliament of Ireland, in which there were many Papists; and in it the sense he had of the way of treating all differences in religion, whether great or small, is thus laid down :—

"Is it not a shame that our two bodies, the church and commonwealth, should exercise mortal hatred (or immortal rather), and being so near in place should be so far asunder in affection? It will be said by each that other are in fault; and perhaps it may truly be said, that both are; the one, in that they cannot endure with patience the lawful superiority of the worthier body; the other, in that they take no care so to govern, that the governed may find it to be for their best behoof to obey: until which time it will never be, but there will be repining and troubles, and brangles between us. This will be done, in my opinion, not by bolſtering out and maintaining the errors and unrulineſs of the lower officers or members of our body, but by ſeverely puniſhing them; and, on both ſides, muſt be avoided ſuch men for magiſtrates and miniſters, as ſeek to daſh us one againſt another all they may.

"And would to God this were all; but is it not a ſhame of ſhames, that men's emulations and contentions cannot ſtay themſelves in matters of this ſort, but the holy profeſſion of divinity is made fuel to a public fire; and that when we had well hoped all had been either quenched or raked up, it ſhould afreſh be kindled and blown up with bitter and biting words? God help us! we had need to attend to this leſſon of Chriſt, 'Learn of me, for I am meek and lowly in heart;' or to that of the apoſtle, 'It behoves the ſervant of God not to contend, but to be meek towards all, inſtructing with lenity thoſe that be contrary affected, waiting if at any time God will give them a better mind to ſee the truth.' 2 Tim. ii. 25.

"And this is my poor opinion concerning our dealing with the Papiſts themſelves, perchance differing from the practice of men of great note in Chriſt's family, Mr. Luther and Mr. Calvin, and others; but yet we muſt live by rules, not examples; and they were men who, perhaps by complexion or otherwiſe, were given over too much to anger and heat. Sure I am, the rule of the apoſtle is plain, even of ſuch as are the ſlaves of Satan, that we muſt with lenity inſtruct them, waiting that, when eſcaping out of his ſnare, they ſhould recover a ſound mind to do God's will, in the place I quoted before.

"But now when men agreeing with ourſelves in the main (yea, and in profeſſion likewiſe enemies to Popery) ſhall, varying never ſo little from us in points of leſs conſequence, be thereupon

Preface.

cenfured as favourers of Popery, and other errors; when molehills fhall be made mountains, and unbrotherly terms given : alas! methinks this courfe favours not of meeknefs; nay, it would hurt even a good caufe, thus to handle it; for where fuch violence is, ever there is error to be fufpected. Affection and heat are the greateft enemies that can be to foundnefs of judgment or exactnefs of comprehenfion; he that is troubled with paffion, is not fitly difpofed to judge of truth."

In how remarkable a manner thefe enlightened views were in harmony with Bifhop Bedell's general principles may be inferred from the following account of his fhare in the Irifh tranflation of the Old Teftament. This letter was written in 1688 by the Bifhop of Meath for Mr. Boyle, when preparing to publifh that tranflation.

"As to the hiftorical account of it all I can add is that in the convocation held at Dublin, 1634, there were no fmall debates about the verfion of the Bible and the liturgy of the church into the Irifh tongue for the benefit and inftruction of the natives; Dr. Bedell, bifhop of Kilmore, being for the affirmative, and Dr. Bramhall, bifhop of Derry, oppofing it. The reafons of the former were drawn from the principles of theology and the good of fouls; of the latter from politics and maxims of ftate, and efpecially from an act of parliament paffed in this kingdom in the reign of King Henry VIII. for obliging the natives to learn the Englifh tongue. However, the reafons of Bifhop Bedell were thought fo fatisfactory that the convocation thought fit to pafs two canons concerning it; the one that the minifter fhould

Preface. xxiii

read the liturgy in Irish, where most of the people were so, (Can. 8); the other for the parish clerk to accompany the minister in reading his part of the service in Irish, (Can. 66.)

"Upon these foundations the pious Bishop Bedell determined to make farther superstructures; and accordingly set himself to the version of the Old Testament into the Irish tongue, taking to his assistance one Mr. King and Mr. Dennis Sheridan, both Irishmen and clergymen, and excellently skilled in the language of their own country, whose office it was to translate the then English version into Irish, whilst the bishop (who was excellently learned in the Hebrew and the Irish languages) revised the whole work, comparing it with the original, and either expunged or added as he saw it nearer or more remote from the original. The work thus happily finished was left by Bishop Bedell with Mr. Sheridan the translator (who survived him), and was by him delivered to the late Bishop of Meath, Dr. Henry Jones, by him communicated to Dr. Andrew Sall, from whom I received it before his death, and gave it to your predecessor, Dr. Marsh; and what fate it hath met with since, he and others whose hands it hath passed can best relate.

"Some part of this narrative I have read in the life of Bishop Bedell, lately published by one Clogy, who is somewhere beneficed in England (if he be alive) and married the said bishop's daughter; what relates to Mr. Sheridan you may receive a more ample account of from the Bishop of Kilmore, who is his son. The title of this Bible as printed; *The Books of the Old Testament translated into Irish by the care and diligence of* Dr. William Bedell, *late Bishop of* Kilmore *in* Ireland, *and now printed for the public good of that Nation.* London."

A point of unexpected interest arises upon the

xxiv *Preface.*

confideration of Bifhop Bedell's intellectual work. May we hope to recover more of his valuable MSS. connected with Irifh ftory. His early biographer, Bifhop Burnet, writing in 1685, ftates them to have been all deftroyed in the rebellion of 1641. But without infifting upon feveral paffages in that valuable life which tell the other way, we have from the careful hand of Dr. Birch, in the Britifh Mufeum, notes made by himfelf of another biography of the Irifh prelate, dated in 1674, which Bifhop Burnet does not feem to have known. Then it is certain that Boyle had the MS. of the Irifh Bible publifhed by him in 1685 from the reprefentatives of the Rev. Dennis Sheridan in whofe houfe the great prelate died. Affuredly the Royal Hiftorical MSS. Commiffioners will find no refearch too careful for the difcovery of the fmalleft finifhed production of this illuftrious Irifh bifhop.

II.

The Sheridans of the 17*th Century.*

Among the beft fruits of Bifhop Bedell's truly apoftolic labours, next to the affectionate homage paid to him by the people of all ranks, were many

Preface.

converfions of Roman Catholic Irifh, fome becoming Proteftant paftors with livings by his lordfhip's gift. Of the laft the moft interefting to us is the cafe of Dennis Sheridan[1] mentioned in the foregoing letter refpecting a tranflation of the Old Teftament into the Irifh language. This excellent man, a progenitor of the family diftinguifhed from his time for rare intellectual qualities, deferves a far more complete notice than can be offered in thefe pages. Under his roof his venerable inftructor and friend was fheltered by him unharmed in the crifis of the rebellion. By his care, too, the learned prelate's MS. was preferved during that cataftrophe to be publifhed a century later by another Irifh worthy, the illuftrious "Chriftian Philofopher," Boyle. The

---

[1] This is the careleffly printed "Heridan" of the dictionary by the Rev. Hugh Rofe, art. Bedell.

"The bifhop, his two fons, and Mr. Clogy were fuffered by the rebels, who had imprifoned them, to go to the houfe of an Irifh minifter, Dennis O'Sheridan, to whom refpect was fhown by reafon of his extraction, though he had forfaken their religion and had married an Englifhwoman. He continued firm in his religion, and relieved many in their extremity."—*Life of Bifhop Bedell by Burnet*, 12mo. ed. by Dove, p. 205.

"The bifhop prevailed on feveral priefts to change, and provided them with benefices; which was cenfured by many as contrary to the interefts of the Englifh nation."—*Ib*. p. 157.

foregoing letter on the MS. connects Dennis Sheridan honourably with that important national work. Moreover, by his own kindly nature as well as from the bifhop's example, the Rev. Dennis Sheridan was the ready hoft to whofe "abode want and pain would ever freely repair;" and whom a countryman as large-hearted, Oliver Goldfmith, might have taken for a type of pure Irifh benevolence. We now have full evidence long fought in vain, for his domeftic tie recorded by Bifhop Burnet, to which may well be traced much of the remarkable career of his fons. Their mother, the Englifh wife of this worthy Irifhman, "a Fofter of good family," would naturally give them fympathies with her own people, without in the flighteft degree weakening their attachment to her hufband and their father's people.

There is no reafon to fuppofe that good early training was wanting to the fons of this hopeful family, two of whom were born in the lifetime of Bifhop Bedell, namely, William, the elder, in 1633, and Patrick, the fecond, in 1638. Both were entered as commoners of Trinity College, Dublin, in 1652, at their refpective ages of feventeen and fourteen. They muft have acquired at home the ufual amount of inftruction to be qualified for ad-

miffion there; and the elder, William, bore the
baptifmal name of the learned prelate.

The youngeft of the three, Thomas, the author
of the work which forms the fubftance of this
volume, was born in 1646. He was entered as a
penfioner in Trinity College, Dublin, in 1660, in
his fourteenth year. Being deftined for the law he
became a ftudent in the Middle Temple in the
year 1670. Profitable employments were however
foon found for him in the Irifh revenue depart-
ments. In Cork he had a poft in the Cuftoms,
charged to him as of the value of more than
9,000*l.*; and he took it with a profit of 4,000*l.*[1]
Before 1677 he feems to have travelled much on
the continent, and in that year he produced the
tract entitled *The Rife and Power of Parliaments*,
here reprinted word for word.

This account of the Sheridan family at this
early period is come down to us in a form at once
authentic and acceptable. It is in a fpeech at the
Bar of the Houfe of Commons in 1680, by this fon
of Dennis, the Irifhman of the old ftock, who allied
his race to England voluntarily by a moft happy
union with an Englifh wife. This eminent fon,

---

[1] Sir James Ware on Irifh Writers, by Harris. Folio, 1778.

when under a grave charge before the House of Commons, vindicated himself bravely in these terms, from the scandal of being a base, paid adherent of the Duke of York, afterwards King James II.

"In clearing myself," he said, "of this aspersion, I must say something, which nought but necessity, that has none and breaks all laws, can excuse from vanity, in that I was born a gentleman of one of the ancientest families and related to many considerable in Ireland. In one county there is a castle and a large demesne, in another, a greater tract of land for several miles together, yet known by our name. I need not say who has the land as chief, —'tis too much, that my grandfather was the last that enjoyed our estate; and that my father, left an orphan at the beginning of King James' reign, soon found himself dispossessed and exposed to the world,—that whole county, with five others in Ulster, being entirely escheated to the Crown. My parents Protestants, —my mother a gentlewoman of England, of good fortune, a Foster, who for my father's sake quitted her country and relations, —both famous for honesty, for their loyalty and sufferings in the late rebellion, when my father escaped narrowly with his life, and at last was forced to fly for relieving and protecting very many English.

"From my birth I had a suitable education. I have some pretensions to letters. I am not altogether a stranger to the Civil Law, nor to the Laws of England, the means intended for my livelihood. But, without my seeking, some friends procured for me the collectorship of the customs of Cork, and the management of most of the inland revenue of that county. This employment, and the incidents attending it, with those of the East

India prizes, and others in the laſt war with Holland put into Kinſale, enabled me to bring 9,532*l.* for my own proportion of advance money to purchaſe the revenue farm of Ireland, as appears of record in the Chancery of England. Being by a brother of mine, without my privity or deſire, led into this undertaking, and a ſtranger to all the partnerſhip, I ſold my intereſt for a profit of 4,000*l.* The money I employed in Corporation Bonds and Church Leaſes, in mortgages and other ſecurities at 10 per cent., the intereſt of that kingdom.

" After this excuſe, if I have no viſible eſtate, I hope no man can doubt but I may live independently, though I happen to be a younger brother. So far from that being a prejudice, it's poſſible to prove to my advantage, being deſigned heir to my two elder brothers, who have not, nor are likely to have, any children.

" I do declare that I neither have nor had any relation of ſervice to the Duke or Ducheſs of York; nor did I ſucceed Coleman in that ſervice.

" For my religion, as I was born a Proteſtant ſo I was bred a member of the Church of England. I have taken the oaths eleven times."[1]

III.

Thomas Sheridan's Tract of 1677.

The character of this tract, put forth at a critical moment without name of author, publiſher, or

[1] State of the Caſe of Thomas Sheridan. London, 1681, 4to. Britiſh Muſeum. King's Pamphlets, No. 100, h. 7.

xxx *Preface.*

printer, yet actively circulated, may be shown in very few words to be even now of great intrinsic interest. Besides a curious historical sketch upon parliaments, the author recommends a single supreme legislation for the three kingdoms; and his electoral reform extends to the " ballot, to avoid heats and secret grudges " (page 27). Quite an original scheme is here also proposed for bodies of *electors* to the House of Commons, intermediary from the " freeholders of every parish, and others if they please," for the choice of a member—a scheme much considered since, in other countries (page 25). He would then have a code of laws made, with a simplification of the courts of justice. Above all, he would abolish all death-punishments, and improve the discipline of all gaols (pp. 34, 45, and 62). He would have judicial censors (page 62); and official historians (page 68). His jealousy of France may be readily passed by (page 114); but what he says (page 29) as to Ireland (page 139) cannot fail to be read with satisfaction in the main (page 139), although much weakened by an expectation of the Irish language being easily suppressed. His views upon taxes, customs, and excise; with his anticipations as to banks and inland bills, with bonds to be negotiated by indorsement

Preface. xxxi

only, and the like, give him the credit of being among the very firſt to recommend changes of law, now never doubted of (146, to the end). As a political economiſt, aſſuredly, if we have outgrown many of his principles, his example proves that in other material points, Adam Smith was by no means the originator of the beſt maxims.

Three topics, elaborately treated in the tract, are at this moment of ſpecial intereſt—namely, a policy of conciliation between Proteſtants and Roman Catholics,—of unity among all Chriſtians; the complete education of all claſſes in common, and the induſtrial employment of the poor. The firſt topic is here examined with a concluſion ſo abſolutely in the ſpirit of Biſhop Bedell's appeal cited above, that the influence of the prelate's work may fairly be held to have traditionally reached Dennis Sheridan's younger ſon, the writer: but that good doctrine is maintained with the powerful logic belonging to that younger Sheridan's original intelligence; whilſt it is ſure to meet in our days with much heartier acceptance than it obtained in the ſeventeenth century.

The ſecond topic, popular education, as here preſented, will have a ſtill more favourable conſideration, in harmony as it is with meaſures on that head which have been prepared by continually extending efforts thefe laft fixty years. On material points Thomas Sheridan is in perfect accord with the moft earneft educational reformers. In truth what we are doing painfully but not hopelefsly, on this gigantic topic, the univerfal education of our people, calls for lights from every fource. The thing is not fo much without good antecedents as many have careleffly fuppofed. A fingle example may be cited, replete with the beft experience to build upon. It is over five hundred years ago that clofe to London, an intelligent Roman Catholic minifter, the rector of Croydon, Richard of Bury, a man famous in his generation, tutor to Edward III. and then his chancellor, declared that " all the nations have hailed the advent of fcience, to be enlightened by her leffons. All, from the fwarthy Hindoo to Arabians, Greeks, and Italians, profpered by her influence awhile and then neglecting her, decayed." Age after age, on this very fpot, great ecclefiaftics were not wanting to act, upon thefe excellent doctrines. They were all popular inftructors. At length, one among them founded a modeft home for induftry in need, and with it a fchool for the lowlieft and the loftieft in common, fully fufficient for the place at the time and long

Preface. xxxiii

after. The Archbifhop Whitgift's endowment flourifhed many a year, but then fhared the frequent decays of "noble poverty," until a palace has fuddenly fprung up in Croydon, to encourage the demands of tens of thoufands, and of a thriving population eager for inftruction in it. Surrounded by a crowd of feminaries of every grade, it is the crowning work, declared by Parliament[1] the other day to belong to all our people together, for their better training, without invidious diftinctions. Rightly adminiftered this old Grammar fchool will receive all and fend forth Thomas Sheridan's "beft capacitated" from the humbleft in wholefome rivalry with the higheft, for the beft culture elfewhere, and thus bridge over the dangerous chafms threatening difcord throughout fociety. Here, as fo often of late, the mifchievous notion of *middle* claffes, has fprung up in forgetfulnefs of every duty. Every where proof abounds, fhowing how correctly the Schools Inquiry Commiffioners have concluded, that to fucceed in the great work of univerfal education, we muft carry the hearts of the people, parents and children, with us; and more than half a century ago in this very town of Croydon, the correctnefs of that conclufion was

---

[1] The Endowed Schools Act of 1869, Preamble.

xxxiv *Preface.*

anticipated in a popular fatire upon the abufe of Archbifhop Whitgift's Grammar School, by making it " a military granary," inftead of " the Univerfity"¹ which it formerly was, to the people's great advantage.

The third topic, the induftrial employment of the pooreft, opens a bold defign for the refolution of perhaps the moft perplexing of all focial problems; how to reduce poverty to a mere claim upon individual pity. This defign is for real work-houfes at any coft, throughout the land, to teach the fuffering, and even delinquent maffes ufeful occupations. The fund for this purpofe was to be, like the Education fund—the adminiftration in both being with the electors chofen by univerfal fuffrage for members of Parliament (page 222).

Thomas Sheridan takes a ftrong view of the falutary influence of thefe combinations; and there are figns at prefent of his judgment therein being put to a large practical teft.

[1] The Devil on Two Sticks at Croydon, printed by T. Harding, High Street, 8vo. 1797, p. 45.

IV.

To this sketch of Thomas Sheridan's tract of 1677 and its antecedents it is not possible here to add such an account of his later remarkable career and writings as can do justice to both. The proceedings before the House of Commons and its committee, upon a highly criminal charge against him, with his successful defence at the Bar of the House, would alone fill another volume. They involve all the intensely interesting questions respecting the plots, real or fictitious, of the time; and even the working of the famous Habeas Corpus Act of the same period belongs to his case. Soon afterwards, in 1688, he re-issued his tract, but with a new title-page only, and the name of a publisher. He was now well known in London; and his "adversaries," alluded to in the speech, had not ceased to trouble him. Bishop Burnet mentions his name with a bitterness not becoming the biographer of Bedell, whose principles were so nobly reproduced by this son of the family beloved by that venerable prelate. It is plain he now looked for high employment in xxxvi *Preface.*

Ireland under King James II. In the correspondence of the day from London to Dublin, his name occurs in that sense.[1] Soon afterwards, he was appointed Secretary to the Government, and made a Privy Councillor in Ireland. Upon intelligence of his intended elevation reaching Dublin, the Earl of Clarendon, then on the point of being recalled, expressed himself in the harshest terms to Thomas Sheridan's discredit.[2] How little this severity was deserved, seems to have been soon shown by the secretary's prudent advice in favour of conciliation between the Irish of different creeds. Notwithstanding, however, his objections to the contrary policy which hastened the ruin of James II.'s cause in Ireland, Thomas Sheridan adhered to the fallen king, accompanying the exile to France. There he wrote a history of the time, which has had the highest praise from the highest authorities—Sir James Macintosh and Lord Macaulay, both of whom have made large use of the unprinted manuscript now preserved in the Royal Library at Windsor.

That work alone justifies Thomas Sheridan's

[1] Sir Henry Ellis, Original Letters.
[2] The Clarendon Correspondence.

assertion at the bar of the House of Commons, in 1680, that he "had some pretensions to letters." It does, and much more. Taken in connection with the widely scattered Libraries of *Stuart Papers*, of which the Sheridan MS. forms a gem, its right appreciation and use may open a field of historical inquiry, vast indeed, but incomparably more valuable than vast. The *Stuart Papers* for many centuries—from the royal captive in Windsor Castle to the royal exile at St. Germains—from Mary Queen of Scots to the fallen Pretender of '45, can reveal enough indeed to condemn, but more to pity the fallen, of whom the whole truth is not yet told.

Above all, these papers from abroad and at home, diligently collected and duly scanned, will reveal at least one "paragon" of the Stuart race, worth erring generations—Henry Frederick, Prince of Wales—"the fame of whose increasing wisdom, stature, favour with God and man, won the hearts of all" in his very boyhood.

These are the words of our chaplain in Venice, addressed to Sir Adam Newton, Prince Henry's tutor, in the year 1607, in his fourteenth year. That chaplain was no other than Dr. Bedell, our "apostolic bishop" of Kilmore, whose correspondent, Sir Adam, recognizes the correctness of this brilliant appreciation of the boy prince.[1]

It is not rash to expect that the Royal Commission upon our Historical MSS. now sitting at the Rolls House, will obtain special inquests into the *Stuart Papers*, wide spread as they are in a hundred repositories at home and beyond sea. The research and its uses will be but a revival of what that exemplar of our young princes meditated a brief space later; and his great name is not without its link with the memory and recollection of Thomas Sheridan, the author of " The Rise and Power of Parliaments."

A high place in the roll of fame may be challenged safely for Thomas Sheridan, the author of this work upon political and social progress. In a most critical period of our history he anticipates vital coming reforms, and advocates ably improvements still wanting. Laborious efforts are now being made to complete electoral and judicial measures which he boldly claimed. In the cause of Christian toleration he preceded Locke; and in that of a milder criminal code, Beccaria and Howard.

---

[1] Original Letters of Dr. Bedell from Venice in 1607. Dublin, 1742, 12mo. pp. 80.

Preface. xxxix

As a financier he was a guide to the founder of the Bank of England, Paterſon; and he may very well have been Adam Smith's inſtructor upon capital points of political economy held to have been ſettled originally by that illuſtrious man. If, as a devoted and enlightened ſupporter of popular education, he only followed Archbiſhop Cranmer and Edward Alleyn of Dulwich, his fine views on that head will be ſtudied with advantage by its more ſuccefsful friends of the preſent day.

The ſingle point on which Thomas Sheridan ſeems to have oppoſed the judgment of his father's venerable friend, the Biſhop of Kilmore, was his neglect of the Iriſh language, of which he expected the ſpeedy extinction (p. 153); and his ſhortcoming on this capital point has had hopeful compenſations. If he undervalued the uſes of that tongue, the joining its ſtudy to other means of enlightening the needieſt Iriſh, would not be refuſed by their later protectors—like Thomas Drummond of Edinburgh, John Muſgrave of county Waterford ("one of the beſt of good men"[1]) Frederick Lucas of Surrey and county Meath. Theſe eminent men had im-

[1] Theſe words were applied to John Muſgrave, of Cappoquin, ſometime Fellow of Caius College, Cambridge, by Mr. O' Connell many years ago to an Engliſh viſitor in Kerry.

Preface.

mediate and more powerful precurfors in their Irifh fympathies, as the late Sir Fowell Buxton, a ripe ftudent in Dublin College, and Archbifhop Whateley.

Nor is there wanting at this moment a legion of patriots among us, as able and eager to promote effectually the moft urgent claims of humanity without regard to condition or creed in Ireland. All of them are obedient to O'Connell's call, which he never withheld from fimilar Britifh and Irifh reforms — oppofed as they are to needlefs and noxious difunion.

The fame union was the object of Thomas Sheridan's afpirations two hundred years ago; and, even in a purer fpirit, Bifhop Bedell before him laid deep foundations for the holy fuperftructure of good-will which, in this nineteenth century fo many of us are ftriving to roufe towards all, but efpecially towards Irifhmen, in even an improved degree, according to our better lights.

The cotemporary biographer of the illuftrious Prelate thus records his good acts along with their obftacles:—

" He would encourage Irifh converts with preferments according to their capacities. When this was noifed abroad, the bifhop was feverely checked by some statesmen, as if he acted contrary to English interest and policy by making the conquered and enslaved Irish capable of preferment in Church and State. That was the portion of the conquering, not of the depressed Irish natives. No man did so much as even attempt this before his lordship. To this he replied, that to leave the Irish hoodwinked and ignorant would be bitterness in the end. To bring them to a saving knowledge of Jesus Christ would be a greater security against all attempts than to found our policy upon Irish blind obedience."[1]

Better is to be done in Ireland, and in Wales, and in the Scottish Highlands, in the matter of human speech, than to attempt ignorantly to destroy it. We can preserve it with infinite advantage. It is a master-key to the hearts of millions of our fellow-men, here and elsewhere. It is the oldest remains of pre-Roman and post-Roman life in these islands and many regions more. The State ought to have

---

[1] "Speculum Episcoporum; or the Apostolic Bishop. The Life and Death of the Reverend Father in God, Dr. William Bedell, Lord Bishop of Kilmore, in Ireland." By his step-son, the Reverend — Clogy. Harleian MSS. No. 6,400. Now published by Messrs. Wertheimer and Co. Paternoster Row. 8vo. 1862, p. 97.

its special schools in all these tongues—not only for young Irish, and Welsh, and Scots, but also for the Manx, and, it may still be, even Cornish remnants. Some, too, of the more apt and refined of our children, British and English, should have careful training awhile in those pure Celtic schools. This system has done good beyond sea. Thus, the families of our missionaries have at once become valuable linguists and interpreters. For example a great success has crowned such works at Natal in the case of an able agent in native affairs in that promising colony, an acceptable communicant with the Zoolu and Basutu chiefs in the Caffre language spoken by millions in all South Africa to the Line. So Lady Raffles' children conveyed their daily orders easily to the Hindoo domestics. So the most pleasing incident in Lord Macartney's often misreported mission to Pekin was the conversation of young Stanton in Chinese with the Emperor Kien-Long. The very wisest act of the Papacy 500 years ago, was its adoption of the design of universal tongue-learning in Rome. It was a humble following of the marvellous gift in Jerusalem when " devout men out of every nation under heaven heard every man his own tongue wherein he was born."[1]

[1] The Acts, xi. 5.

Preface. xliii

Assuredly all this may serve as a profitable lesson to us, with our responsibilities of world-wide empire, instead of letting slip our power by want of will to guide it. What would our universal travellers, the sons of Queen Victoria, have given to be able to speak with the Red Indian, the Hindoo, the Chinese and Japanese, the Basutu, the Australian, and New Zealander, whom each of them in turn has visited!

Add to this Divine gift of tongues, which we may easily command, that other means of communicating great lessons of humanity to the untaught coloured man which the genius of a colonial governor devised two generations ago, only to be disregarded by the home authorities. It was making the eye do the sterner work of the ear and tongue —the artist teach the true uses of life better than the hangman.[1]

[1] Appendix.

June 1, 1870.

CONTENTS.

ERRATA.

Page xxxv. line 13, *for* " 1688" *read* " 1685."
Page 30, line 18, *for* " That it is idle" *read* " It is idle."
Page 246, line 7, *for* " remain for more diligent" *read* " remain much for diligent."

VIII. Of Liberty, Property, and Religion . .	70
IX. Of Liberty, Property, and Religion (*continued*).	89
X. Of Liberty, Property, and Religion (*continued*).	96
XI. Of Liberty, Property, and Religion (*continued*).	102
XII. The Intereſt of England in reference to France . . .	114
XIII. Of Taxes .	146
XIV. Of Trade	181

CONTENTS.

	Page
PREFACE, newly writ by the Bookseller's Friend	xlix
THE PUBLISHER TO THE READER	lxix
CHAP. I. The Introduction	1
CHAP. II. Of the Rise and Power of Parliaments	6
III. Origin of Government	8
IV. Origin of Government (*continued*).	25
V. Of Laws	34
VI. Of Laws (*continued*).	45
VII. Of the Courts of Judicature	57
VIII. Of Liberty, Property, and Religion	70
IX. Of Liberty, Property, and Religion (*continued*).	89
X. Of Liberty, Property, and Religion (*continued*).	96
XI. Of Liberty, Property, and Religion (*continued*).	102
XII. The Interest of England in reference to France	114
XIII. Of Taxes	146
XIV. Of Trade	181

Contents.

APPENDIX.

		Page
A. Proofs of Thomas Sheridan's authorſhip of the Tract of 1677		241
B. Pedigree of the Sheridans of the 17th century	. .	242
C. The Ulſter Cuſtom illuſtrated	. .	243
D. Biſhop Bedell's printed Books and MSS	. . .	244
E. The Stuart MSS. at home and abroad	. . .	246

A

DISCOURSE

ON THE

RISE and POWER

OF

Parliaments,

OF

Laws, of *Courts* of *Judicature*, of *Liberty*, *Property*, and *Religion*, of *Taxes*, *Trade* and of the *Interest* of ENGLAND in *Reference* to FRANCE. In a *Letter* from a *Gentleman* in the *Country* to a *Member* of *Parliament*. .

Salus Populi Suprema Lex esto.

LONDON,
1677.

PREFACE,

NEWLY WRIT BY THE BOOKSELLER'S FRIEND.

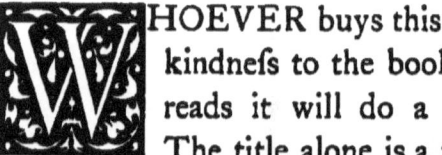HOEVER buys this tract will do a small kindness to the bookseller; but he that reads it will do a greater to himself. The title alone is a temptation to invite one to look into it in this time of disorder; but if wit and learning, reason and piety, the knowledge of men and deep consideration of government signify anything, the discourse is a perfect snare to captivate the reader. And it hath one advantage peculiar to itself to detain him, that he will meet with many things there which no man ever writ, or perhaps thought on before.

The novelty alone will gratify the men of pleasure and curiosity; and, as for the grave and the wise, that chain of reason and good nature which

Preface.

runs through it, will make them scratch and think twice before they condemn it.

It was written to a member of the last Parliament about Christmas last was twelve-month, and since that time has crept abroad into the world, and is now made more public, as well for the general as the bookseller's particular good. But a great change of affairs happening in this interval, it is fit to acquaint you that the author never dreamt of the horrid plot, which has been lately discovered, when he pleaded for toleration to honest and peaceable Dissenters. He measured other persons by his own candid temper, and did not think there could be found a sect of men who would endeavour the advancement of their religion by shedding the blood of their prince, in an age when rebellious principles and their abettors have received such confutations as they have in this, both by God and man.

But Truth doth not vary with time, how much soever some persons may abuse it. I cannot persuade myself but that liberty of conscience is a natural right which all men bring with them into the world; for we must all give an account of ourselves to God, and stand or fall by our own faith and practice, and not by the religion of the state or country where we happen to be dropt.

Preface.

It is impossible for men to believe what they lift, or what others would have them, though it should be beaten into their heads with beetles. Persecution makes some men obstinate and some men hypocrites; but evidence only governs our understandings, and that has the prerogative to govern our actions.

The design of Christianity is to make men happy in the other world; and in order thereunto, it teaches them to regulate their passions, and behave themselves with all sobriety, righteousness and piety in this. The doctrines whereby this is enforced are so few and so plainly delivered, that they are at this day acknowledged by all the several sorts of Christians that make a number, or are fit to be considered under a name in the world. For how many are there who do not profess the Apostles' Creed? which was the old rule and measure of Christian faith, unalterable, unreformable, from which nothing ought to be taken, to which nothing need to be added, as Irenæus and Tertullian declare. And if men would be persuaded to preserve these ancient boundaries of Christianity inviolate, and suffer the primitive simplicity to be restored, the great occasion of squabble and contention would be cut off; and they would not dispute for ever about a lock of wool, or the knots of a bulrush; but inftead of being extremely learned in trifles, and extremely zealous for moonfhine, they would grow kind and charitable, and lay afide their unreafonable cenfures of one another.

Aquinas and Bellarmine, and the *Synopfis purioris Theologiæ*, would not be ftudied fo much, but the Sermon on the Mount a great deal more; and upon cafting up the account it would be found that what we loft in fubtilty thereby we fhould gain in religion.

St. Hilary, the famous bifhop of Poictiers, has an excellent faying to this purpofe, " Non per difficiles nos Deus ad beatam vitam quæftiones vocat, nec multiplici eloquentis facundiæ genere folicitat; in abfoluto nobis et facili eft æternitas; Jefum fufcitatum à mortuis per Deum credere, et ipfum effe Dominum confiteri."[1] God doth not call us to heaven by underftanding abftrufe and difficult queftions, nor invite us by the power of eloquence and rhetorical difcourfes; but the way to eternal happinefs is plain, eafy, and unintricate; to believe that God raifed up Jefus from the dead, and to confefs him to be the Lord of all. The fenfe of this

[1] De Trinitate, lib. 10, *circa finem.*

Preface.

will soften the minds of men, and dispose them to mutual compliances and forbearances; and then we shall not think it needful by severities, and penalties to compel others to go to heaven in our way with great uneasiness, when we are resolved, they may with safety and pleasure get thither in their own.

Upon these grounds the wisest emperors in Christendom have allowed liberty to Dissenters, as Theodosius did to the Novatians, who had separate churches at Constantinople, and bishops of their own persuasion to govern them, and enjoyed all the privileges of Catholic Christians.

And the opinion of King James sent to Cardinal Perron, in the words of Isaac Casaubon, will be remembered to his honour, whilst his name shall be known in the world as the best resolution which was ever given of this question. "Rex arbitratur rerum ad salutem necessariarum non magnum esse Numerum, quare existimet ejus Majestas nullam ad ineundam concordiam breviorem viam fore, quàm si diligenter separentur necessaria à non necessariis, et ut de necessariis conveniat omnis opera insumatur in non necessariis, libertati Christianæ locus detur."[1]

[1] Epist. Isaac. Casaub. epist. cccxvi. pag. 385.

Preface.

The king is perfuaded that there is no great number of things neceffary to falvation ; wherefore his Majefty believes there will not be met with a fhorter way to peace than that diftinction be carefully made between neceffary things, and thofe that are not fo; and that all pains be taken for agreement in neceffaries, but that allowance be granted for Chriftian liberty in thofe things that are not neceffary.

This is not a demand which has been only made of late, fince the Chriftian name has been fo fcandaloufly divided as it is at this day ; but it is that which the primitive Chriftians pleaded for as their right and due, that they ought to be tolerated, though they were miftaken, fo long as they were peaceable.

To this end Tertullian made an addrefs to Scapula, the governor of Africa, and tells him, " Humani juris et naturalis eft poteftatis unicuique quod putaverit colere, nec alii obeft aut prodeft alterius Religio. Sed nec Religionis eft cogere religionem, quæ fponte fufcipi debeat non vi. Cùm et hoftiæ ab animo libenti expoftulentur. Ita etfi nos compuleritis ad facrificandum, nihil præftabitis Diis veftris; ab invitis enim facrificia non defiderabunt, nifi contentiofi fint; contentiofus autem Deus

Preface.

non eſt."¹ It is the right of mankind and a natural privilege to worſhip according to what he believes. One man's religion doth neither good nor harm to another; it is no part of anyone's religion to compel another man to be of the ſame with him, which ought to be undertaken freely, not by compulſion, even as the ſacrifices are required to be offered with a willing mind; and therefore, though you compel us to ſacrifice you will do no ſervice to your own gods; for they deſire no offerings from the unwilling, unleſs they be quarrelſome; but God is not contentious. Lactantius² has ſpent a whole chapter to ſhew the unreaſonableneſs of perſecuting men for religion, and that violence is an incompetent argument to propagate truth. St. Chryſoſtome³ makes it a mark of hereſy, and argues thus; doth the ſheep perſecute the wolf? no, but the wolf does the ſheep. So Cain perſecuted Abel, not Abel Cain. Iſhmael perſecuted Iſaac, not Iſaac Iſhmael. So the Jews perſecuted Chriſt, not Chriſt the Jews; ſo the heretics do to the orthodox, not the orthodox to the heretics; therefore by their fruits you ſhall know them.

¹ Tertull. ad Scap. cap. 2.   ² Lactant. lib. v. c. 20.
³ Chryſoſt. Homil. 19 in Matth.

lvi   *Preface.*

The truth is, the perfecuting practice was firſt introduced among the Chriſtians by the fiery and turbulent ſpirits of the Arian heretics, who had corrupted the Emperor Conſtantius,[1] and brought him to their party, and then made uſe of this power to confute the Catholic biſhops and their adherents, by baniſhment, impriſonment, and confiſcation of goods. Againſt which unworthy proceeding, Athanaſius[2] inveighs with great reaſon and vehemence, as a preparation for the coming of antichriſt. But when this poiſon was once caſt into the church, it was but a ſhort time before the founder and ſincerer part of Chriſtians was infected with it; and as their intereſt grew at court, ſo they made uſe of it to baffle their adverſaries and retort their own arguments upon them, obtaining laws to be made againſt ſeveral heretics, with very ſevere penalties, the loſs of goods, of liberty, the power of making a will, and in ſome caſes, the loſs of life. Which laws are yet upon record in both the Codes of Juſtinian and Theodoſius.[3] But though by this means they prevailed at laſt to ſuppreſs the hereſies which troubled the Church, yet the beſt and wiſeſt

[1] Sulpit. Sever. lib. ii. c. 54, 55, &c.
[2] Athan. Epiſt. ad Solitarios.
[3] Cod. Juſt. l. i. tit. 5, de Hæreticis, &c. Theod. 2. 5.

men amongst them disapproved the expedient, and thought it unreasonable to purchase the establishment of truth by such rigours and by the shedding of blood.

The first instance which I remember of any capital sentence formally pronounced against any dissenters, was against Priscillian and some of his followers; but then St. Martin, the bishop of Tours, interceded with all his might to hinder the proceeding; and Sulpitius Severus gives an ill character of the fact, when he says, "Homines luce indignissimi, pessimo exemplo necati, aut exiliis necati."[1] It was of ill example and a scandal to Christianity, that they were banished or put to death, though they did not deserve to live. And when a band of soldiers was sent to suppress a conventicle of the Donatists (who were very numerous and extremely troublesome in Africa), and bring them to Church, Parmenian objected the Armatum Militem, and the Operarios Unitatis to the Catholics, as an unseemly and an unworthy practice. And it cost Optatus[2] a great deal of pains to write almost a book to wipe off the imputation; which he could not do, but by denying the fact as a calumny

[1] Sulpit. Sever. lib. ii. c. 65.
[2] Optat. cont. Parmen. l. i. c. 3.

whereof the Catholics were not guilty, and disagreeable to the doctrines of their meek and peaceable Master.

St. Austin has declared his opinion how the Manichees were to be treated in such favourable and gentle words, as shew he was not pleased with the law in force against them. Cod. Just. tit. 5, de Hæreticis: leg. Manichæos: "Illi in vos sæviant qui nesciunt, quo cum labore verum inveniatur," &c.[1] Let them be rigorous against you, that do not understand what pains is required in the discovery of truth; and with what difficulty errors are avoided; let them be severe against you, that know not how rare and hard a thing it is to conquer carnal representations by the serenity of a devout mind. Let them rage against you, that are ignorant with what labour the eye of the inward man is cured, that it may be able to behold its own sun; let them be cruel towards you that know not what sighs and groans are necessary to the understanding of God in degree: in fine, let them be angry with you, that are free from all such mistakes as they see you deceived with. But for myself I can in no wise be severe against you, for I ought to bear with

---

[1] Aug. contra Epist. c. 1, 2.

Preface. lix

you as with myself, who was once one of you; and treat you with that patience and meekness as was shewn to me by my neighbours, when I was furiously and blindly engaged in your erroneous doctrines.

Salvian, a priest, and as some think a bishop of Marseilles, has manifested the like candour and meekness towards the Arians. "Hæretici sunt, sed non scientes: deniq; apud nos sunt hæretici, apud se non sunt," &c.[1] They are heretics, but they are ignorantly so; they are heretics in our esteem, but they do not think so themselves; nay, they so firmly believe themselves Catholics, that they defame us with the title of heresy. What they are to us the same we are to them; we are certain they injure the divine generation by saying the Son is inferior to the Father; they think us injurious to the Father, because we believe them equal; the honour of God is on our side, but they believe it on theirs; they are undutiful, but they think this the great office of religion; they are ungodly, but this they believe is true godliness; they err therefore, but they err with an honest good mind; not out of hatred but affection to God, believing that

[1] De Gubernat. Dei, lib. v. pag. 142.

they both love and honour the Lord. Although they want a right faith yet they are of opinion that this is the perfect love of God; and none but the judge can tell how they are to be punished for the mistake of their false doctrine in the day of judgment.

This was the soft and charitable spirit which breathed in those eminent defenders of Christianity, who were so zealous for their religion, as to suffer for it themselves; but not so furious as to make others suffer to promote it. They had another method of propagating the truth; in meekness instructing those that oppose themselves. For, indeed, the only proper punishment of the erroneous is to be taught.

Having discoursed thus far concerning indulgence towards Dissenters, *i. e.* for charity, righteousness and peace; and that every one has a right by the great charter of Nature to make the best provision he can for his own happiness; I foresee the envy to which this way of reasoning will be exposed; as if it opened a gate to all sorts of sects and foolish opiniators, even to atheists themselves; and stript the magistrate of that power whereby he is enabled to attain the end of government, that the people under him may lead quiet and peaceable lives, in all godliness and honesty.

Preface.

I know so much of human nature and the extravagant follies of mankind left to the conduct of their own passions, that these would be the certain consequences of unlimited liberty to all persons; and therefore I plead not for it. My notion of liberty precludes all the inconveniences in this objection. It is not a natural law which is unchangeable, but a natural right only for a man to choose what religion he will profess. And there is no right of Nature, which I know of, but what is limitable to the public good, and forfeitable by the abuse of it.

A man may forfeit the right which he has to life, which he holds by Nature as well as to his estate, which he holds by law. An atheist, a murderer, &c. may as justly be killed as a viper or a wolf, or any other noxious animals; because they have done irreparable mischief to the commonwealth already, and prevent doing more for the time to come. The natures of such persons are greatly degenerated, and it is but reasonable that they who have lost the common virtues should likewise lose the privileges of mankind. And I judge the like concerning the liberty which every man has to inquire into the truth of several systems of religion, and publicly to maintain that which

Preface.

appears to him established upon the surest foundations.

When it is apparent that religion itself is damnified, the safety of the government endangered, and the peace of the Commonwealth broken by any sort of doctrines, the persons professing those doctrines have forfeited their natural freedom, and ought to be restrained.

Accordingly, first, no man is to be allowed to publish impieties which evidently tend to the dishonour of God and wicked life; as that God doth not take care of the affairs of this world; and that there are no rewards and punishments in the other; that there is an indifferency in human actions, and no good or evil antecedently to the civil constitution, &c. For the truth in these cases is so plain by the light of Nature, and by the manifold discoveries which God hath made, that no man who seeks for it with an honest mind, but may discern it; and accordingly errors of this nature are not to be ascribed to weakness of judgment, which is to be pitied, but considered as proceeding from malicious principles and tending to base ends, and so are punishable as corruptions in manners. This sort of men indeed are not within the limits of this question,

Preface. lxiii

for they have no confcience, and therefore can challenge no privilege from it; and no government can have fecurity from men of no confcience, and therefore cannot be blamed if it do not protect them. And, feeing they oppofe the confent of mankind in fuch momentous affairs, why fhould they not forfeit the benefit of human fociety? and if the fword were oftener drawn and fharpened againft them, it might poffibly reconcile fome perfons to the authority, who are now no great friends to it, nor altogether of St. Paul's mind, that the minifter of God bears not the fword in vain, but is a punifher of evil doers, and a praife to them that do well.

Secondly, no man can claim any right to freedom whofe doctrines tend to the deftruction of government in general, or the diffolution of that which is eftablifhed. For the benefits of government are fo great, (though like thofe of health, they are not fo fenfibly difcerned by any thing fo much as by their abfence) that all mankind have been contented to purchafe them, by parting with fomething out of everyone's ftock, to maintain a common arbitrator of differences, and a common defence from injuries. And the alterations of any particular form, or the removal of any particular perfon, in whom the government is fixed, is always attended with fo many certain inconveniences; and, if with any, fuch uncertain advantages, that ordinary prudence ought not to truft fuch perfons whofe religion leads them to anarchy or to change. Nay, fubmiffion to government is fo incorporated into all religions of the world, natural, Pagan, Jewifh and Chriftian, that it is impoffible anyone can reconcile religion with the oppofition to the prefent government: therefore all fuch doctrines as thefe,—that dominion is founded in grace; that it is lawful to depofe heretical princes, or vindicate the true religion by the fword; that an idolatrous king may be cut off; that the original of power is in the people, and upon male adminiftration and tyrannical government, they may refume their firft grant; are to be difcountenanced in every commonwealth, and the abettors of them to be reftrained and punifhed, unlefs the rebels of England have fome peculiar privilege, and they that ought to be hanged in every other nation under heaven, have a particular charter to be indulged as the godly party here.

Thirdly, he that will not allow the fame liberty which he afks, deftroys the right to his own demands; he is of a narrow perfecuting fpirit; in love with his own dear felf, proud, conceited, and an enemy to the reft of the world.

For, I pray, are we not all equal by nature, have you more of the image of God, or a less share of original sin than I? You tell me that I am an idolater; and cannot I say that you are a heretic? You are certain, if God's Word be true, and the Spirit of God do not deceive, you are in the right; I say you are very confident, and Solomon tells us, "The fool rageth and is confident." I took not up my religion upon trust, I have read the Bible and the ancient writers, the most indifferent arbitrators of differences in religion; I have consulted the wisest men, and heard all parties speak; I have prayed to God for his assistance, that he would guide me into all truth, and I verily think God has answered my prayers; and it is you, not I, that are in the mistake. But, because there may be no contention between us, I am contented to compromise the quarrel, and we will dwell together charitably with united affections, though with different judgments. But you cannot in conscience accept of this fair offer; you have a command to the contrary. Come out from among them and I will receive you; be not unequally yoked with unbelievers; have no fellowship with the unfruitful works of darkness, but rather reprove them. You have a promise to depend on, and you look up to God to perform it.

Preface.

Behold, I will make them of the synagogue of Satan which say they are Jews, and are not, for they lie; I will make them to come and worship before thy feet, and know that I have loved thee. Well, sir, I am sorry my tender of peace is so scornfully rejected, upon the misapplication of such texts of Scripture as equally and indifferently serve all parties, or are nothing to the present purpose; you must not be angry if I strike the first blow, rather than suffer you to take your own opportunity to knock me on the head.

When the cause comes to be tried, before equal umpires, you will be judged out of your own mouth that challenged liberty, which you would not grant; for you have transgressed the great rule of righteousness, not to do to others what you would have done unto yourself. Upon these terms the pretences to liberty are destroyed. But if the wisdom of any state shall confine their indulgences to pious, obedient, and charitable Dissenters, I cannot perceive the prejudice which difference in speculations and disputable points can do in religion, or the power of the magistrate.

But at the same time I cannot but admire the admirable temper and moderation which is shown in the church and government of England; that requires nothing neceſſary to ſalvation, but the acknowledgment of the ancient creeds; that teaches nothing but what is pious and charitable; whoſe liturgy is grave, wiſe, and holy; whoſe rites are few and material; whoſe laws are full of candour and compliance, allowing freedom to any five Diſſenters together to worſhip God, in their own way: whoſe true ſons and ſubjects are the greateſt favourers of Chriſtian liberty which are in the world; and I pray God to give all people that diſown it wiſdom to underſtand it.

THE PUBLISHER TO THE READER.

HAVING, I muſt own, not without pleaſure, read the following papers, and believing they might in ſeveral inſtances —I do not ſay all—give ſome ſatisfaction to others, and contribute to the public good, for which I perſuade myſelf even thoſe notions that ſeem moſt odd and impracticable were intended, I reſolved to make them public, but was checked again by calling to mind that he from whom I in ſome ſort extorted them obliged me not to diſcover him. Nevertheleſs, conſidering I might do the one without the other, I purſued my former reſolutions, yet taking this further care that even the printer ſhould not know from whence they came. And now let me tell you, whatever you ſhall think of this diſcourſe, it is the iſſue of a ſober brain, though perhaps a little too much inclined to humour and unfaſhionable rigid virtue, and not ſo agreeable or ſmooth as you would have had it if my friend had

THE PUBLISHER TO THE READER.

HAVING, I muſt own, not without pleaſure, read the following papers, and believing they might in ſeveral inſtances —I do not ſay all—give ſome ſatisfaction to others, and contribute to the public good, for which I perſuade myſelf even thoſe notions that ſeem moſt odd and impracticable were intended, I reſolved to make them public, but was checked again by calling to mind that he from whom I in ſome ſort extorted them obliged me not to diſcover him. Nevertheleſs, conſidering I might do the one without the other, I purſued my former reſolutions, yet taking this further care that even the printer ſhould not know from whence they came. And now let me tell you, whatever you ſhall think of this diſcourſe, it is the iſſue of a ſober brain, though perhaps a little too much inclined to humour and unfaſhionable rigid virtue, and not ſo agreeable or ſmooth as you would have had it if my friend had dreſſed it for the eyes of any other beſides myſelf to whom he ſent it ſheet by ſheet, and having writ it in leſs than eight of the laſt holidays, you may believe, had I allowed more time, it would have come, even to me, reviewed. As it is, I make it yours, and aſſure you, whatever cenſure you paſs upon him or me, we ſhall both be unconcerned; as complaiſance made it mine, ſo a good intention of ſerving my country makes it yours. For myſelf, I do not aim at being richer or greater; the patrimony left me ſatisfied and invited my unambitious mind to the retirements of a private life, which I have made eaſy by innocent recreations, company and books; it was not my own ſeeking that I am now placed in a more public ſtation, wherein, though perhaps I have done no good, yet I am pleaſed I never did any hurt, having always purſued without paſſion or intereſt whatever my conſcience, the beſt rule and ſevereſt judge of men's actions, convinced me was beſt.

As to my friend, he is one has read ſome books and more men, thanks God he is that which the world calls a fool—a good-natured man—one that heartily loves all mankind, and has ſo particular a zeal for the good of his country that I believe he would ſacrifice his life to ſerve it. But almoſt despairing that ever things will be better than they are, and finding by what he has seen abroad that a man may live more happily in England than in any part of Europe, and now grown old, by temper more than years, he has resolved chiefly to mind himself, whom, to enjoy more fully, he has bid adieu to all thoughts of business, to which, having never been bred by any calling, he has had the more opportunities of considering all, of improving himself, and observing most sorts of men; and, as a speculative philosopher, to the entertainment of himself and friends, he passes very free remarks on all actions and things he judges amiss; and, being biased by no manner of interest, I am persuaded he speaks his conscience; and he has the good fortune to make others often conclude he does not only speak a great deal of truth, but also further satisfies them that it is much easier to find faults than mend them, that there ever were, and ever will be, disorders in all human societies, that there are fewer in that of England than in any other, and that they are there more curable.

Thus much I thought fit to tell you to prevent any misapprehensions concerning the persons who are the occasion of this trouble or diversion, call it what you please.

Chapter I.

THE INTRODUCTION.

Sir,

HAD you only commanded me to have given you an account of the Laws and Cuftoms of another Utopia, an Ifle of Pines, or of O. Brazil, though unfit even for fuch a tafk I would not have difputed it; but finding you have impofed upon me, who am neither ftatefman nor merchant, a neceffity of playing the fool, by treating of England's policies and trade, I confefs I could not without great reluctance comply with fo fevere an injunction.

I have always been averfe to difcourfes of this kind, which in private men are no

Introduction.

farther tolerable than as idle philosophers, to pass away their vacant hours in such otherwise useless speculations; and in them, too, I have heard such oftener condemned than commended; the authors esteemed foolish and impertinent, troublesome or dangerous; and some, we know, by indulging themselves too much in this vanity, have straitened, if not wholly lost their liberty and fortunes. We live not in Plato's Commonwealth, but *in fæce Romuli*, where a full reformation of laws and manners seems only to be wished, not to be obtained without a miracle. Why then should any, especially the unconcerned, busy their heads with what they cannot mend? 'Tis much more pleasant, and safer far, to let the world take its course, to believe that in the regular stated motion of nature things are so ordered by Divine Providence that they will not, cannot suffer themselves to be ill-managed. Nature, if we hearkened to her dictates as well as religion (which we equally despise), would convince us it were our duty (I am certain it would be our interest, our

Introduction.

happiness even in this life) to submit quietly to the powers above and their ordinances, because all powers are of God.

Thus I acknowledge every private man ought to think and do; but public persons, that is to say, law-makers, are to consider they were born not only for themselves, but for the good of others; and therefore are obliged to exert that power with which they are intrusted, for the joint common good of the people, without partial regards or private ends.

If they would sincerely mind this, and if our hot-brained state mountebanks, who being but private men yet quarrel at every thing that is not conformable to the capricios of their own wild fancies, would cease to intermeddle in their superiors' province, England might be the happiest kingdom of the world; whereas the contrary practice rendered her not long since the seat of civil wars, tyranny and confusion, and has at present so filled her with murmurings and repinings, jealousies and fears, that she which formerly gave law

Introduction.

to others, and was a terror to more than Europe, is now in danger to become weak and contemptible in the eyes and opinions of her neighbours.

These, and such like, were the considerations that made me so long resist your command; to which I had never yielded, but to prevent the loss of your friendship, with which you so solemnly threatened me in your last. Take then, in the same order you prescribe, the best account I am able in so short a time, to give to your several following particulars of the Rise and Power of Parliaments; of Laws; of Courts of Judicature; of Liberty, Property and Religion; of the interest of England in reference to the designs of France; of Taxes and of Trade. But you are to observe, that what I write is with as much liberty and little care as people discourse in Coffee Houses, where we hear the state affairs of all nations adjusted, and from thence guess at the humour of the people and at the times.

In this, therefore, you are not to expect any studied phrases or elaborate connections,

Introduction. 5

close, neat transitions, &c. Your servant (whom I conjure you by the strictest ties of friendship not to discover), has neither will nor leisure for such a work, which being intended only for your closet, you may be content to take in a plain English dress.

Chapter II.

OF THE RISE AND POWER OF PARLIAMENTS.

THE great and many revolutions and changes which in all places have attended human affairs, and the particular inundations of the Romans, Saxons, Danes, and Normans into this kingdom, together with the ignorance and carelessness of former ages, have left us in so much darkness and uncertainty, that I think it not only difficult, but morally impossible to trace out exactly the beginnings of things. If it be so then in all affairs, we may cease to wonder why men are so much at a loss in their inquiries into, and debates of the present matter, viz. of the Rise and Power of Parliaments, which has received very different forms and shapes according to the interest and power of the feveral contending parties. This makes me think its true face can never be fully difcovered, though perhaps it may be uncertainly gueffed at by fome lines, faint fhadows, and ftronger probabilities gathered from the fcattered memoirs of monks, who cannot well be fuppofed impartial, efpecially in ecclefiaftical, nor full in the relations of ftate affairs, in the accounts of which they did not hold themfelves concerned. But yet they are the beft guides we have, for from the ancient Rolls in the Tower one cannot believe there was any exact diary of things, or if he do, muft conclude many are fpoiled by the injury of time, omitted through negligence, or made away for private ends. However, we may yet pick out of both this truth, that though the rife of Parliaments, like the head of Nilus, be unknown, yet they have been of long ftanding and of great power.

Chapter III.

ORIGIN OF GOVERNMENT.

AND we shall find it reasonable they should be so, if we look back into the grounds and origin of Government, which we may suppose to have been introduced by the general consent and agreement of as many families as upon the increase of mankind joined in one common society; divided the earth into particular proportions; and distinguished between *meum* and *tuum*. To this they were induced by love, not fear, which is but the consequent of reason convincing them that the enjoyments of life were thus best served and promoted;— and because that being, and well-being could not be continued or enjoyed but by the society of women and the products of labour, and that, if some would be idle, and many

Origin of Government.

covet the same woman, the great design of nature, happiness, founded on living well and in peace, might be perverted into the state of misery, war. To prevent the two necessary consequences, poverty and death, they entered into mutual compacts, articles, or laws, agreeable to that great and fundamental law of nature, riveted into their beings, to do as they would be done unto. That is, they resolved, agreed, and promised one another to be guided by the rules of reason, or, which is one and the same, to continue men. But, because it was probable some, yielding too much to their passions, might swerve from this great rule, and so wrong others as well as themselves, therefore, that no man might be judge and party, they unanimously confirmed to the elder person the continuance of that right which nature had given him over the fruit of his loins during its minority, to determine whatever differences should happen—believing him, as the common father of the family, to be most impartial, and as the longer experienced, the wisest man.

This power, though great, exceeded not the limits of their then-enacted laws in the true and natural meaning, which they took care to make very few and plain, that all disputes and intricacies (not only the disturbers, but destroyers, of justice) might be avoided.

And finding they were not only liable to danger at home, but from abroad, from such other societies as had already or might afterwards set up for themselves, and that it was not possible for all to watch against these dangers, they therefore resolved to put that care into the hands of one man; for which great undertaking the coward as the fool, if those two really differ, were equally unfit—inconsideration in the one being what fear is in the other, a betraying of the succours which reason offers. Nature, then, by giving their judge most authority, wisdom, and conduct, which, with true courage—the effect also in a great measure of experience—are the great qualifications of a general, designed him for that honour; which the people readily con-

Origin of Government.

firmed, promising obedience, and investing him with the power of making war and peace, both, at his instance—reserving to themselves the liberty of examining and approving the reasons; which the great and wise captain judged convenient, knowing that without the consent of all, he could not but want the assistance of some, which might disable him to defend himself or them, whereupon the ruin of the whole must inevitably follow.

And because the prince's whole time must be employed in this great work, part of which was the preparing his son for the succession by instilling into him the necessary seeds, the principles of virtue, religion, wisdom, courage, munificence, and justice; the people willingly agreed to entail upon him and his successors a certain excisum, or proportion of every man's labour, answerable to the occasions of the public, and to the particular state and grandeur necessary for the support and maintenance of his authority and reputation.

But because a greater proportion was needful for extraordinary accidents, as of war, &c.

they set apart annually another quota, to remain for such uses in a kind of public bank, so to be ordered as might greatly increase their common treasure, and do good to the poorer sort of labourers and tradesmen, and maintain in hospitals, such impotents or aged persons as should be disabled to make provisions for themselves.

The revenue they made great enough, as well as certain, that the prince might not lie under any necessity of contriving from time to time new artifices and ways of raising money, that great rock of offence on which they foresaw no prince could stumble without vexation, animosities, and hatred; not only discomposing the happiness, but occasioning the overthrow of any state. And so the people, being sure of the remainder, they proportioned their expense to their gettings; the former they moderated, not only by prudent sumptuary laws, but by the hazard of their reputations, esteeming it infamous not to lay up yearly something of their labours; by which course the public taxes became easy; which they made perpetual, that their children should be under a necessity of following their examples of thrift, and so might likewise be insensible of the burden; foreseeing that taxes imposed upon people who are so far from saving aught, that they account themselves good husbands if they do but yearly make both ends meet, beget ill blood, murmuring and discontent; crying that the bread is taken out of their mouths, or the clothes from their backs, which are often followed by the evil consequences of rebellions, and the subversion of the Commonwealth. For such never consider that their own extravagance made those imaginary needs, which, when they happen, are no otherwise to be removed but by moderating former expenses.

Thus they wisely contrived, and interwove the perpetuating the subject's safety and the prince's dominion, never secure but when founded on mutual love and confidence. I do not find the practice of this policy anywhere so well continued as in the states of

Venice and Holland; which has preserved the first about twelve centuries, and made the latter increase so prodigiously in less than one.

Now, because they foresaw the products of their labour would exceed their expenses, and that the remainder would be useful for commutations with their neighbour for some of their commodities, but that in driving this trade they would be exposed on sea to piracies, &c.—to make their navigation safe, they agreed, that the public for securing them should receive by way of premium or insurance, a certain excisum out of all things exported or imported, which we now call customs.

And, lest the too great desire of wealth should make them forgetful of their duty to God, their parents, and their country, that is to one another, they ordain'd that a sufficient number of the elders of the people, grave, sober, discreet persons, should, at certain times set apart for that purpose, remind them of their duty in every of those particulars; and also instruct their children in the laws of

Origin of Government. 15

God and of their country. And becaufe the tending of this work would take up a confiderable portion of their time, they allowed falaries to thefe public officers, out of the common ftock. In thofe days of innocence, when art was not interwoven with religion, nor knavery with policy, it was an eafy matter to be pious and juft; and if the higher powers were pleafed to remove thefe two, we fhould foon again fee that golden age. The duty of both tables was comprifed in few articles; that to their neighbours confifted as now, in doing as you would be done unto; that towards God (of whofe being they were convinced by the ftrongeft of demonftrations, the confideration of the vifible things of the world), in thankf-givings and adorations, the effect of gratitude to the Author of their being and of all good things, in believing the immortality of the foul, and of its being fufceptible of rewards and punifhments in another life, and in the confequence that fin is to be repented of. Thefe were their common fentiments, the dictates of nature; the substance of which was acknowledged by all, even the most barbarous of nations, and therefore could not be the inventions of policy, the dreams of melancholy men, or the effects of education. These are the opinions of the unthinking, and therefore wild and loose, and were the wishes formerly of the few debauched; but the great, sober and wise philosophers of all ages, upon the exactest scrutiny, finding them to be the impresses of nature, as essential to our being as light to the sun, pronounced the speculative atheist an impossible thing. And because they were sensible that a liar, as destructive of the very being of human society, ought to be banished the commonwealth, the first of their laws and the cement of the rest was, that every man should not only speak truth to his neighbour, but stand firm to his promises. And knowing that laws, though never so good, would prove insignificant if not duly observed, and that some men would never be wise, that is, would never consider, and consequently would not

Origin of Government. 17

eafily be reftrained from folly, from offending; to deter the flavifh and inconfiderate, they did not only annex certain penalties to the breach of the laws, but unalterably decreed that no offender, though never fo powerful, fhould efcape the punifhment.

Thefe penalties were pecuniary mulcts, lofs of liberty, bodily labour to the public, or banifhment. The power of life and death they would not give, becaufe they could not transfer that to another which was wanting in themfelves; the taking away of life was peculiarly referved by nature as its own indifpenfable right, as moft reafonable becaufe fhe alone could give it. They confidered that terrors are but affrightments to duty, that corrections are for amendment, not deftruction, which courfe fhould they have purfued, they might accidentally have run themfelves into a ftate of war; fince nature had told them it was not only lawful but neceffary, if they could not otherwife preferve their own, to take away the beings of any that attempted theirs;—that it would be againft the end of society, mutual happiness; this rendering the sufferer incapable of all, to which therefore he neither could nor would have consented. This or something not unlike it was, I persuade myself, the form and substance of the first commonwealths, which if you narrowly look into, you may perhaps find some lines that drawn out fully, might be no ill model for any commonwealth.

And, to come nearer home, it has some resemblance to what for several past ages this kingdom did and does now enjoy. To omit the British times, of which we have but very thin gleanings of the Druids, their oracles of learning, law and religion; and to skip over that of the Romans, who were never able perfectly to introduce their manner of commonwealth, we shall find that in the time of the Saxons, (a people of West Friesland, so called from the shape of their sword, a kind of scimitar,) and in that of the Danes, the manner of Government was as now in substance, though not in form or name, by king and parliament; but whether the Commons were called to this great assembly or no, I cannot find from the imperfect registers of elder times. One may guess they were originally members of it because the same people in West Friesland, from whence they descended, do at this day continue a form of government, different from all the rest of the provinces, not unlike this. There are sufficient proofs that the peers, that is, the chief of the clergy and best estated gentry, were as often as the king pleased (for it was originally *edicto principis*) summoned to consult with him of the great affairs of state. Which council was before the Conqueror's time called by several names, as *Concilium* absolutely, sometimes the epithets of *Magnum*, *Generale* or *Commune* were added; it was often known by the name of *Curia Magna* and others, and was composed *ex episcopis, abbatibus, ducibus, satrapis et sapientibus regni;* among which if any will say the Commons had place I will not dispute, because in those times, when titles of honour were not the arguments of good fortune, or the marks

Origin of Government.

of the prince's favour, the king called to this great council such as large poffeffions, courage or wifdom recommended as fit; for we find that the father's having fat there, gave not right to fuch fons as did not with their eftates inherit their virtues.

It appears farther, that the great council in the later end of the Saxons' reign, and till the beginning of King John's, had, by the grace of kings, accuftomed themfelves, without any fummons, to meet thrice every year, at Chriftmas, Eafter, and Whitfuntide; which courfe was not interrupted by any particular fummons, but when in other feafons of the year the public occafions required their meeting. The long continuance of the Barons' Wars made the before-ftated meetings of the great council return to the uncertain pleafure of the Prince.

Whatever the power of the Commons was before the Conqueft, it plainly appears that for fome time afterward their advice was feldom defired, and as things were then ordered, their confent was not thought neceffary, being always included in that of the Lords: for the Conqueror having fubjected the natives to an entire vaffalage, feized upon all their poffeffions, referved to the crown large proportions in every county, gave part to the Church in frankalmoigne, and the refidue to his fellow adventurers in the war, to be held by knight fervice. Thefe fubdivided part of theirs to their followers, on fuch conditions as rendered them perfect flaves to their mafters, rather than their lords. By the poffeffion of fo much power, thefe barons or freeholders (for the word fignified no more) did what they pleafed with their vaffals and became very terrible to the Conqueror and his fucceffors; to curb whofe extravagance though all were willing, King John was the firft that made the attempt; but, by his over haftinefs, he gave birth to the lafting broils of the Barons' Wars. He, with defign to fupprefs the too great power of the Lords, in the fixth year of his reign, about a war with France, called

Origin of Government.

for the Commons' advice and counsel with the Lords, which had been done above one hundred years before by Henry the First, who in his reign summoned them twice—at his coronation, and in his eighteenth year. The next time after King John, that we find them summoned was in the forty-ninth year of Henry the Third's reign, whose summons appears upon record; so that he may be said to have perfected what Henry the First and King John designed, making the Commons a part of that great judicature which they have ever since continued, and for some time after, in one and the same house.

It was usual in those days to mention in the writ the cause of assembling this council. In a summons of Edward the First, a wise, just, and therefore a fortunate prince, concerning a war with France, in the seventh year of his reign, these words are observable, "Lex justissima providâ circumspectione stabilita, ut quod omnes tangit ab omnibus approbetur," much better sense than Latin.

Succeeding kings have been pleased to

Origin of Government.

confult in Parliament of all the high and great concerns of the ſtate, of what nature or kind ſoever. The conſulting thus with the whole body of the people, was firſt the grace or policy of kings; and the practice was always ſucceſsful to thoſe that uſed it, as the contrary proved deſtructive: for the kings, having by this courſe gained their ſubjects' hearts, found it eaſy to command their purſes and their hands.

This great repreſentative of the Commonwealth, the Parliament, confiſting of three eſtates, viz., the Lords ſpiritual and temporal, and Commons with the King as head, you will with me eaſily conclude, may do anything within the reach of human power.

You muſt pardon me if I wave anatomizing the diſtinct powers of the ſeveral parts of this great body; whoſoever firſt attempted that, deſigned the overthrow of the beſt conſtituted government in the world, where the king wants no enſigns of monarchy or majeſty, where the people have not only all the freedom, liberty, and power that in reason can be wished, but more than any of their neighbours enjoy, even than those in the so much more cried up but little understood commonwealth of Holland, where they have liberty in name, but in reality are very slaves and beasts of burden.

Chapter IV.

THE ORIGIN OF GOVERNMENT, *continued.*

NOW, whether the way of convening parliaments might not be altered into the following (or some other more equal than the present seems to be), I leave to themselves to determine, *viz.* That every parish, freeholders and others, if they please, should meet and choose two honest knowing men, on whom their power of electing members should be devolved; this done in every parish, the several twos to meet and choose two for the hundred; that agreed, the respective twos of every hundred, at the time and place appointed, to choose the members out of such as are resident in the country, both knights and burgesses. Nor does it seem very reasonable that the later should exceed the former, especially considering that many of the ancient boroughs are decayed, and yet the number raised by the additions of new ones, beyond what it was before; but by this manner of election that inconvenience, if any, will not be considerable. To every two members a sidesman to be chosen, who should duly attend at the place of sessions, and that he might be prepared in the absence of both, or either of the members, they should make him master of all that passed from time to time in the House. And that every person elected might serve the public without private consideration, the electors or a justice of peace, in their presence, to administer an oath framed to this effect: " That in all proceedings they endeavour to inform themselves fully of the state of the matter and therein act according to conscience, without particular interest or design; that directly, or indirectly, on the account of their vote or serving, they shall not receive by themselves or others any reward or gratuity whatsoever." On breach of this oath to be liable to all the penalties of perjury. It is not to be doubted but the honour of promoting their country's good (that giving a fort of immortality which all men covet), will invite gentlemen enough sufficiently qualified to undertake this work on these conditions, how hard soever they appear. It is not reasonable that parliament men should be maintained or rewarded (unless in praise and statues) at the country's charge; to do it gratis is all the real good they do the commonwealth, in which as private men their interest, and consequently their gain, is greater than that of the meaner sort. The elections to be by the balloting box, to avoid heat and secret grudges.

Nor would it be useless to add, that all things be carried fairly and openly in the House; that the debate of anything proposed be adjourned to the next day's meeting; for in the time of rest, upon our bed, our night's sleep does change our knowledge, and qualify the effect or cause of passion, inconsideration; that every member by himself or sidesman be constantly present, under severe penalties to the public; that nothing be put to the vote but in a full Houfe, not of forty (who cannot be the major part of above four hundred, and therefore at firft was fure a trick), but of all the members; nor then carried by majority till the reafons of every fingle diffenter be examined, the diffenting perfon convinced, and in cafe of obftinacy after conviction (of which in fo wife an affembly none can be fuppofed guilty), expelled the Houfe. The queftion not to be re-affumed till after the election of a new member, unlefs his fidefman be of a contrary opinion in the debate. It is poffible the fwaying argument was at firft but one man's, whofe credit and authority might prevail upon the reft, without examining his reafons; which makes it prudent to weigh the force of what is offered againft it. By the contrary courfe they may, by this they cannot, fuffer, fince reafon or truth is always one and the fame, and however difguifed by the fophiftry of wit, it muft at laft overcome. Thus by proving all things and holding faft that which is beft, they will ac-

Origin of Government.

quit themselves to the present and succeeding ages. Such manner of proceeding would silence all murmurings and clamours—" that the Parliament is divided into factions, a court and a country party; though the interest of the one be not directly opposite to that of the other, yet the members, for ends of their own, honour or rewards, do make them so; of this they are convinced by seeing some turn cat in pan, appearing strongly in one session for that which in a former they as vigorously opposed—and by observing others to compass elections by faction and interest, by purchase or covinous freeholds; that contrary to several acts of parliament, members living in the south are chosen for the north, and therefore are, to the injury of the people, as much strangers to the affairs of the places for which they serve, as those two points are distant from each other—that they pass laws, witness that against Irish cattle, &c., not for the common good, but to show their interest and power to mischief a man they hate, or to revenge some received or supposed injuries or affronts—that therefore it is necessary to dissolve this as not being a free parliament, and to call a new one—that to do so frequently is most agreeable to reason and to former statutes; and to that end several causes are prepared to put a difference between the two Houses, in point of jurisdiction," &c.

But such as more seriously weigh things may, I hope, be convinced these are the groundless surmises of some, and false suggestions of others, discontented and ill-disposed persons, the old disturbers of our Israel's peace, who, delighting to fish in troubled waters, endeavour once more to put all into a flame of tyranny and confusion, to see what fish they may by that treacherous light bring to their own nets. That it is idle to imagine the court, the best refiner of wit and language, should not have as piercing a foresight as the country; that being allowed, they must be sensible of the fatal consequence of a divided house or kingdom, their loss is at least as great as any others, their all is at stake; it is therefore contrary to their intereſt which never lies conſequently to their practice to endeavour parties. It is irrational, no leſs than ſcandalous, to conclude, becauſe ſome men's ſenſe, by ſecond thoughts and fuller conſideration of things, is altered, that therefore they are bribed; as if perſonages of ſo much honour, wiſdom, and public-ſpiritedneſs, could be induced by any ſiniſter practices or bye-reſpects to betray their country and entail upon themſelves and their poſterities more laſtingly than they can their eſtates, great and inexpreſſible calamities. And can it be ſuppoſed the miniſters have ſo little underſtanding as not to foreſee that the taking off violent members any other way than by conviction of their errors were endleſsly to increaſe their numbers, and, hydra-like, by cutting off one head, to give occaſion to the ſprouting up of many. Nor is it leſs abſurd to believe the Parliament, when they find the conveniences, the reaſon of ſtatutes ceaſed, will not repeal them. It is no affront to their judgments nor to their loyalties ſo to

Origin of Government.

alter with the times; an obftinacy in the contrary refolution would indeed be a difparagement to their underftandings. It is to be hoped the wifdom of the Parliament is fuch as not to quarrel for trifles, after the manner of women or children; that they will lay afide all partial regards, and, without heats or perfonal reflections, intend the great work, the common fafety, recollecting that they were the home-bred divifions more than the Conqueror's forces, that occafioned Harold's overthrow, and England's entire fubjection to the French. Even thofe very men who invited William, fuffered in the ruin—fo juft and natural it is to love the treafon and hate the traitor. Does not every man know that the power of whole France is greater than that of a part, that of Normandy, could be? Duke William cannot be fuppofed to have been more watchful to feize the prey than Louis is, who perhaps has fet thofe very men, at leaft their leaders, on work, that openly pretend moft to oppofe his defigns; while, in the meantime, by fowing underhand difcords and fears among the people, they beft promote his purpofes. It is no unheard-of practice for politicians, as well as watermen, to look one way and row another; but I hope no cunning Achitophel will be able to divert the Parliament from the great bufinefs of this conjuncture.

Chapter V.

OF LAWS.

WHEN they have done that, I wiſh they would think it worth their labour to look into the laws, and obſerve what of them is fit to be repealed and what continued. The happineſs of a ſtate conſiſts in a regular form of government, by juſt and equal laws, few and plain, fitted to the moſt ordinary capacities; theſe qualifications are as neceſſary to the well-being of the people as that of promulgation was ever accounted to the eſſence of a ·law. But ſuch is the fate of England that the laws are almoſt numberleſs, which makes them impoſſible to be remembered; and, what is worſe, are ſo very intricate that they may more reaſonably be looked upon as the devices of cunning men to entrap the ſimple, than as

Of Laws.

the rule by which all are to fquare their actions and their lives; and what is yet worfe, they were never promulgated, though provided for by thofe ftatutes that enact the reading of fome of them in cathedrals at leaft once a year, and of others four times. Is it fit or juft men fhould be punifhed by laws they neither know nor can remember? There is no one entire body of laws; that of the ftatutes is fo tedious (and fome yet remain in the Parliament Rolls not printed) that it can hardly be read over in a month's time; though an hundred times reading will not enable a man to remember them, and yet he may fuffer for not obferving what he has not read, or if he had, could not remember. But what is the greateft evil,—if they could remember they could not underftand; fince the very judges, who have not only been bred at the feet, but are themfelves the Gamaliels of the law, and much more,—are wont to fpend whole terms in the reconciling and expounding of particular ftatutes. And it often happens that after thefe long advifements they being divided in their opinions, the parties concerned, wearied in those toils, endeavour after all their cost and labour to quit their right, or impatiently expect the making of new and more intelligible laws.

These great disorders have been occasioned by several conspiring accidents,—length and warping of time, crooked interests of some lawyers, and the continual wars, foreign or domestic, with which this country has been harassed, I might say, since the invasion of the Romans, &c. But to come nearer our own times, since the Conquest, since the first making of these acts, England has not enjoyed one half century an entire peace; to which unhappiness I know not whether the vexation of the law or bigotry of religion has contributed most. I do not doubt but in other ages they were as sensible of the evil as we are in this, but the same accidents continuing, rendered it remediless. Edward the Confessor regulated the Saxon laws, but his care proved of little advantage after the coming in of the Conqueror; who, designing

Of Laws.

to set up a new form more agreeable to the customs of Normandy, or his own will, made himself deaf to the people's desires of being governed by the rules of that holy prince, who was deservedly sainted no less for his zeal and love of justice in matters of law, than for his strictness of life in those of religion. From the Conqueror's time downwards there have been attempts of this kind almost in every king's reign; but the wars and divisions and consequently dissolutions, that often happened between the kings and their parliaments, sometimes lords, sometimes commons, about the liberty of the subject or prerogative of the crown, (not without good reason concluded to have been set on foot by the crafty lawyers, by this time grown considerable,) prevented bringing to pass the intended reformation of the law. I will not insist upon all the kings' reigns where this was designed, nor go farther back than Henry the Eighth's time, when ingenious Sir Thomas More was by him set on work to frame a model; but the succeeding accidents frustrated that attempt; the troubles and revolutions that continued during the reigns of Edward the Sixth, Queen Mary and Queen Elizabeth, hindered this work, which at wife Burleigh's advice was refolved on by the latter queen. The learned King James determined to finifh it, and the knowing Sir Francis Bacon was pitched upon to frame a fcheme of new laws or model the old; but the difcontents about religion, with the greater artifice of the lawyers, then more numerous, diverted that glorious enterprife.

Some living were actors, others fpectators, of the troubles that have fince happened, which gave way not to a reformation but confufion of the laws; and yet the Long Parliament (or rather Conventicle) knowing their great and good mafter purpofed it, refolved upon a new method of laws. But the idol themfelves had fet up, as a juft reward of their treafon, prevented this by turning them out of doors with their beloved Magna Charta, treating it and them with fovereign contempt. Too many in other countries, no lefs than this, have wholly loft their freedom by endeavouring to enlarge it beyond law and reafon; as it has alfo fometimes befallen ambitious princes, who, ftriving to augment their power and dominions beyond the boundaries of juftice, have, inftead of new acquifts, forfeited their ancient and lawful poffeffions. The gardener's afs in the apologue defigning to mend himfelf by changing mafters found at a dear-bought experience none fo kind as the firft; the obfervation of the evil of thofe days has given us reafon to believe that wifdom beft which is learned at the coft of others, and to remember the wife man's advice, meddle not with thofe who are given to change. This I fpeak as to the fundamentals of the government, which can never be altered by the wit of man but for the worfe; but the fuperftructures of hay and ftubble are grown fo cumberfome and rotten that they are fit for nothing but the fire.

Though I am far from giving credit to any prediction or prophecy but thofe of Holy Writ, yet I cannot but remind you of that old Latin one, *Rex albus*, &c., on which you know our wishes taught us to fix a pleasing interpretation. This hint will bring to your mind, what perhaps has not been there almost these thirty years, that both for his innocence and the accidental snow that fell on his hearse, the late King Charles was that "white king," who for some time was to be the last in England; that afterwards his son should, from beyond the seas, return to the possession of his crown, and that in his days, religion and laws should be reformed, and settled, upon the eternal foundations of truth and justice. The fulfilling of this prophecy now will seem as miraculous an effect of providence as that of our sovereign's restoration, and will as much eternize the wisdom of the parliament as the other their loyalty. What remains of this undone, we might hope to see finished, as old as we are, if they would be pleased to espouse it heartily, and defend themselves against the noise, wranglings and opposition of the lawyers and clergy, who are no more to be consulted in this case than merchants concerning exchange, &c., because, as the wise Syracides observed, their interest would bias them: "There is," saith he, "that counselleth for himself; beware, therefore, of a counsellor, and know before what need he hath, for he will counsel for himself."

There was law before lawyers; there was a time when the common customs of the land were sufficient to secure *meum* and *tuum*. What has made it since so difficult? nothing but the comments of lawyers, confounding the text, and writhing the laws like a nose of wax, to what figure best serves their purpose. Thus the great Coke, bribed perhaps by interest or ambition, pronounced that in the interpretation of laws, the judges are to be believed before the Parliament. But others, and with better reason, affirm, that it is one of the great ends of the Parliament's assembling to determine such causes as ordinary courts of justice could not decide.

The laws of England are divided into common and statute laws; the common are ancient customs, which, by the unanimous and continued usage of this kingdom, have worn themselves into law. Statutes are the positive laws of the land, founded on particular accidents and conveniences not provided for by the common law. Civil and canon law are of no force, but as they are incorporated into the body of one or other of these laws, if either may be called a body which has neither head nor foot, for they lie scattered in some few books, Bracton, Littleton, Glanville, Fleta, Coke, Plowden, Dyer, Croke, &c., their commentaries or reports, or rather in the arbitrary opinion of the judges or some celebrated lawyers. For nothing is in this trade certain or regular, what one gives under his hand for law, another gives the direct contrary; judgments and decrees reversed, as if that could be just one day that is unjust another; and why in England must law and equity be two things since reason and conscience in all other parts of the world are one and the same? and why cannot laws be so plainly worded as that men

Of Laws.

of common fenfe may, without an interpreter, difcover the meaning? if they be not fo ordered, fpeedy and exact juftice will at beft be retarded. But you will tell me there would be no need to complain if men would follow Chrift's advice: "If any man will fue thee at the law, and take away thy coat, let him have thy cloak alfo;" the reafon was fo plain, that it was needlefs to exprefs it, viz., left the lawyer fhould come between and ftrip you naked, even of your fhirt. This, you fee, is prudence as well as religion, as indeed all Chrift's precepts are in the very affairs of this world. Whatfoever was true of the Jewifh lawyers, the prefent practice of fome of ours renders them obnoxious to the cenfures of the fober and the curfes of the paffionate; moft men agreeing, that to go to law is like a lottery, or playing at dice, where if the game be obftinately purfued, the box-keeper is commonly the greateft winner. But fince fome men will be fools or knaves, why fhould not the few honeft be as much fecured as poffible?

Of Laws.

When the Parliament have fettled the laws, I wifh they would think of fome more fitting reftraint of offences, than what the penal ftatutes direct almoft for every crime—the lofs of life. If we examine the feverity of this practice, we fhall find it contrary to the law of nature, the pofitive law of God, Thou fhalt not kill, and ineffective of the intent of laws,—amendment. Self-prefervation is the chief defign of nature; to better which, not to deftroy it, was the ground and end of government and laws; which makes it contrary to reafon that any means fhould be made or declared fuch, which were deftructive of the end for which they were made.

Chapter VI.

OF LAWS (*continued*).

IF then the loſs of life, as it moſt certainly does, puts an end to all earthly happineſs, it is evident that it never was, nor ever could be, judged an inſtrument productive of that end; perhaps it may be ſaid, that this may be true of every ſingle man, as ſuch; and yet may be falſe when conſidered with reſpect to the whole, as a member of the ſociety. I anſwer, it cannot be true in the latter, if falſe in the former; becauſe we muſt believe that at firſt every man conſidered what was abſolutely beſt for himſelf, without any reſpect to another, on whom he cannot be ſuppoſed otherwiſe to look than as he was or might be ſubſervient to his own particular and immediate happineſs. And ſince the whole is made up but of ſeveral individuals, it muſt be granted that every one of them had the fame confiderations: and fince it was not in the power of any to transfer that right to another which nature had denied to himfelf, we may then fafely conclude, it is againft the law of nature, *i. e.* againft reafon, to believe that the power of life or death, by confent of all, without which there was no law, could at firft be vefted in any fupreme power; and that the ufing of it does naturally put us into a ftate of war, the evil becaufe directly deftructive of happinefs, defigned to be avoided. This is a truth implied in the law of England, not only by binding the criminals to reftrain their warring, but alfo by the punifhment inflicted on the *felo-de-fe*, which fuppofes no man to have power over his own life, as certainly he muft have had if he could have given it to another. Nor will the difficulty be removed whether we derive government either of the other two ways; paternal right, or the immediate gift of God; for parents had no fuch power by nature, in the ftate whereof we are all equal.

Of Laws.

We are little more obliged to them for our being, than to the influence of the fun, both as to us are involuntary caufes; that which binds children to an indifpenfable duty of gratitude, is the parents' care in providing for their well-being, when they are unable to fhift for themfelves, and their giving them virtuous education (that which is of all, the trueft obligation), than which nothing is among us more neglected; which has made fome at the gallows, not without caufe, take up the advice of Job's wife againft God, firft curfe their parents and then die. Children may indeed be ungrateful, which is the worft or the all of crimes, but parents cannot revenge this by death without being unjuft; becaufe there ought to be a proportion between the crime and the punifhment, and a warrantable authority in him that inflicts it, which in this cafe are both wanting; for ingratitude, theft, rapine, and what ever elfe is practifed by the wicked, are in themfelves reparable, and the fufferer may in an equal meafure be compenfated for his lofs, for *bona fortunæ* or the goods of fortune are exterior to us, and confequently accidental, and when we are defpoiled of them by any, we have full fatisfaction by a reftitution in fpecie, or in value. This courfe is the meafure and fquare of all civil contracts; for if I detain wrongfully the money you lent me, I am compellable but to repay you. Why then fhould it be capital, to take your horfe without confent, when either reftitution, or a punifhment more commenfurate to the offence may be had? As for the authority of the punifher which muft be warrantable, it is plain the father has no fuch over the children, who in the ftate of nature are equal with him; for fince he gave not the being, he cannot legally take it away, and for the act deftroy the agent; punifhment being defigned, not only for the terror of others, but for the amendment of the offender. To deftroy then the laft, that fuch as are guiltlefs may continue fo, is to my apprehenfion a piece of the higheft injuftice. Befides, no prince claims a right over the fubject's life,

Of Laws.

what ever he does to his crown, otherwife than by the pofitive laws of the land, which fuppofe the man himfelf to have given that power by his confent, which is already proved impoffible. Therefore, we may conclude, the inflicting of death is againft the pofitive law of God, who has referved this to himfelf, as a peculiar prerogative, and although he has allowed the rulers of the earth to fhare in his titles, yet left they fhould intrench on his honour (of which he is very jealous) by exceeding the bounds of reafon, he immediately fubjoins, but " ye fhall die like men," to put them in mind that they were to act as fuch. It cannot then be fuppofed that human conftitution can make that juft which the Almighty declares unlawful. He that does fo, fets himfelf up above all that is called God, deftroys moral good and evil, makes virtue and vice but only names, which if allowed, we may bid farewell to the people's and prince's fecurity; for this roots up the very foundations of peace on earth, as well as joy in heaven.

Of Laws.

Nor will it serve to say this was practised in the Jewish commonwealth; that was God's own peculiar province, and he that was sole author of life might dispose of it at his pleasure; and though every part of that economy be not accountable, yet it is not without good grounds supposed, because the Jew's happiness or misery seems to have consisted in the enjoyment or want of temporal blessings, that the taking away life here was in lieu of that punishment which sinners under the Gospel are to receive in another life; and unless human laws might as immediately be called his, and that every magistrate were a Moses, I could not believe it lawful for them to follow that example, especially considering that they do not write after this copy in the punishment of all crimes. I will not make comparison in many, yet I cannot but take notice that idolaters and inciters to it were there punished with death, while among us atheism and irreligion do not only go free but the professors of those admirable good qualities pass for wits

Of Laws. 51

and virtuofos; drunkennefs and gluttony are efteemed as marks of good breeding, computing the abilities of our brains by the number of bottles our ftomachs can hold; this vice among the Jews was accounted fo ridiculoufly filly that they could not believe it was poffible for men grown to the ordinary years of underftanding to be guilty of it, and therefore we find no punifhment allotted but for children, viz., that if drunken or gluttonous children did not by the parent's admonition and correction learn more wit, that then their parents were obliged to bring them forth and teftify their folly, and with the congregation ftone them to death.

But this abominable childifh crime, the mother of all imaginable wickednefs, has among us no punifhment; or what is the fame, if not worfe, none inflicted.

As to the third part of the affertion, viz., that the lofs of life is ineffective of the intent of the law,—amendment; this will appear true by obferving, that men whofe loofe education has made it their intereft to wifh there were no other life, by often wishing and never considering, come at last to be fools; and with them to "say in their hearts, There is no God; we have no way to live, thanks to our good parents or our country, but to rob or steal; as for the next life, if there be any such thing, let that look to itself; let us provide for this; a short one and a merry; who knows but we may escape seven years? and that is the age of a man; if we are taken and cannot get a pardon, it is but a few minutes' pain, and there is an end." Thus these foolish wretches discourse themselves to the gallows, on which did you but know the vast numbers hanged for some years last past, you would quickly believe that sort of punishment rather makes more, than frightens any from being, thieves, robbers, or other criminals. In the eastern monarchies the greatest emperors, the Turk himself, though always in war, fancy some kind of art or trade, and by this do not only divert themselves but by their examples more powerful than any precept oblige the people to so necessary a practice. The ladies,

Of Laws.

even the greateſt, of all other countries have callings too, and ſpend not their whole days in making and receiving viſits, or in preparations for them,—exquiſite dreſſings. If by ſuch a courſe, or any other, people were induced not to live in idleneſs, none would be under a neceſſity of ſtarving or breaking the laws as many now are. And if afterwards any were ſtill found guilty, a puniſhment likely to prevent others, and do a further good to the public, would be to take away the names of all criminals that "they may be no more had in remembrance," put them into a common livery, a fool's coat, red and yellow, keep their heads continually ſhaved, their foreheads ſtigmatized with marks diſtinguiſhing their crimes, and their eſtates forfeited to increaſe the prince's revenue; condemn them to public workhouſes, mines, or galleys. The labour and toil, the hard fare, and the diſgrace, would deter more than death; and, as ſome believe, be more agreeable to the dictates of nature, to the law of God, and to the profit of the commonwealth. In cafes of murder the public lofes too much by the flain; it will not fetch him back to fend another after him. Why then fhould they think themfelves fatisfied for one lofs to have it doubled upon them by another? But fuppofing (which I never can allow) that reafon requires life for life, can it think it equal to fet the life of a man but at a fhilling? Is a horfe or a cow, a fheep or a deer, or a lefs thing, a cock or a hen, an equal price for a man's life?

And yet for perjury he fuffers but a pecuniary mulct or lofs of ears. Why fhould not he that fwears falfely at leaft have his tongue cut out? In the Jewifh law the perjurer was to fuffer the fame kind of evil that he brought upon his neighbour; and at this day among the Perfians and Indians a liar is not only deprived of honour but of all further fpeech. Had it been thus enacted among Chriftians, the falfe tongue and the lying lips would not have deftroyed fo many men's lives and fortunes. But if we will not, after the Jewifh and Roman manner, bring in

Of Laws.

reparation or the *lex talionis*, which with them was practised in other cases besides that of felony, let us at least make some further provision for the security of man's life, let it be put out of the power of one witness, observing that great law that said, "At the mouth of two witnesses or three shall he that is worthy of death be put to death, but at the mouth of one witness he shall not be put to death." What I seem to say paradoxically on this subject, I would have you understand as I intend it, of the first societies of mankind; and you may likewise further observe, that though custom and the positive laws have made punishment by death the practice of all nations, yet with humble submission to my superiors, I persuade myself, it was introduced by absolute power among the heathens, and since continued among Christians, because they did not fully consider that a better way might be found for correcting and avoiding crimes.

Having now provided against death upon the account of any crime, it may well enough confift with the king's mercy and goodnefs (which invite him to be tender of the lives of his fubjects), to determine pofitively never to grant a pardon or remittal of the punifhment to any criminal, though never fo great a perfon. In Edward the Third's time it was enacted that " no pardon fhould be granted out of Parliament;" I wifh it might gracioufly pleafe his Majefty, with his Parliament, to enact further, that no pardon fhould at any time be granted; than which I am fure nothing would more contribute to the perfect obfervance of the laws.

Though our laws cannot, yet an entire execution of them in their utmoft feverity may, be as unalterable as thofe of the Medes and Perfians; which courfe would prevent the many ill effects the hope of pardon does now daily occafion, though there never were fewer granted; yet fo long as there is any ground of hope, the debauchee is encouraged to go on in his folly, and none being particularly excluded, he reckons himfelf not incapable of that grace.

Chapter VII.

OF THE COURTS OF JUDICATURE.

BUT now admitting that the laws were never fo good, if they be not duly and equally adminiftered by the feveral courts of judicature, the evils do ftill remain. To prevent which great inconvenience, fuch has been the happy contrivance of England's conftitutions, that the fame power that gives the law cannot only pronounce it (in fpite of Coke's affertion to the contrary), but has alfo determined that it fhould be a part of its own power, to call all inferior courts and officers, juftices of the peace and others, to a ftrict examination how they have fquared their actions and proceedings to the rule they have given them; from which, when they are found to deviate, it

Courts of Judicature.

would be for the advantage of all, that the Parliament would exert its ancient power in regulating the many abuſes crept into inferior courts. Into which if there was ever need of looking there is now at this day when the complaints are loud; by which, perhaps, molehills may be made mountains; yet all this ſmoke cannot be without ſome fire. This I have been told for certain that their judgments are founded as much upon rules or interpretations of ſtatutes of their own pleaſure, introduced by the intereſt of lawyers and officers, as upon the ſtrict letter of the laws, in which your education, though not your practice and your long obſervation, has made it ſuperfluous for me to particulariſe the many irregularities in the adminiſtration of juſtice, which would fill a large volume.

But to begin with the courts, I think it were convenient that each of the four at Weſtminſter ſhould be reduced to their ancient practice, and not ſuffered to encroach upon one another, to the ſubject's great vexation, who often quits his cauſe rather than follow it through all the mazes of the several courts, where at last after some years tossing by writs of error, &c. from post to pillar, if his money does but hold out to make the lawyers that sport, he may sit down by his loss, or have recourse to the arbitrement of two honest neighbours, which at first had been the speediest and cheapest way of justice.

In ancient days the King's Bench intermeddled only with the pleas of the crown; but now an *Ac etiam*, ushered in by a feigned assertion of force and arms, and by supposing the defendant to be in *custodia marescalli*, or the plaintiff privileged some other way in that court, robs the Common Bench, whose jurisdiction even by Magna Charta is of all common pleas between party and party. The Common Bench, by practice of attorneys not to be behind hand, has likewise of late days introduced an *Ac etiam*, and several debts or promises are supposed, with intent to bind the subject to special bail, whereas I am confident it cannot either by common or statute law be evinced, that anciently special bail or a *capias,* before actual summons was in any action required; and that, therefore, it is a mere invention to get money and to vex and impoverish the subject.

The Exchequer was only to hold plea of such actions where the plaintiff was really indebted to the king (and perhaps too, not able otherwise to pay it), or where the parties were by their privilege to plead, or to be impleaded in that court. But now, by falsely suggesting they are indebted to the king, and not able to pay him but out of the thing in demand, they are suffered to sue in that court, alleging a *Quo minus,* &c. in their declaration. But before such irregularities were introduced, it was not so much law, as honesty, prudence, and skill in arithmetic, that were the necessary qualifications of the barons; in which court a chancery was erected to moderate the rigour of the fines and amerciaments estreated into that court, and to extend to the king's debtors those favours which the barons could not show. The causes then remaining for the

Courts of Judicature. 61

high Court of Chancery, were the penalties and forfeitures between man and man, which at common law were due, and all other caufes, that for want of evidence were no where elfe tryable. But fuch have been the mighty contrivances of the practifers in that court, that they have found out a way for the trial of all caufes there, where notwithftanding a man's pretence in his bill, that he wants witneffes (though that be but a trick to entitle the court to the action) after he has obliged the defendant to fwear againft himfelf, contrary to the common law, and that of nature, *Nemo tenetur prodere feipfum*, which feems to be the pofitive intent of Magna Charta, he takes out a commiffion to examine witneffes. In the civil law the complainant, if required, is obliged as well as the defendant, to fwear the truth of the bill; and fure that is as fitting to be done in the king's great court of equity and confcience, as in the ordinary courts of juftice in other nations. Nor would it be amifs, that all witneffes fhould in that court, as well as others, give their testimony *viva voce*, and that there should be some unalterable rules, both for the officers of the court and the clients; since conscience and right reason are always the same and unalterable; which would prevent the reversing of decrees (a tacit confession they were unjust), and other inconveniences, too many to be recounted; only one is so notorious I cannot pass it by,—the assuming a power of impeaching judgments at common law, which the statute declares to be premunire.

Another practice as inconvenient as any, is, the judges giving too great an authority to a former judge's report or opinion. It were to be wished that in the rest of the courts, the present practice of the wise Lord Chancellor Finch were observed, who, considering that a report is founded upon such reasons as are not with the report conveyed to us, that only stating in brief the matter of fact; and that the case is alterable by any one accident, rightly infers " that no report but the reason of the present case squared to the rules of the law, ought to guide his judgment."

To this may be added that in every court there should be a settled number of clerks, attorneys and lawyers as well as judges: that these how just soever, should not continue above three years in any one court. Whatever the sheriff's power was formerly, sure I am, that exercised by the judges exceeds what now they are possessed of; and yet the wisdom of former ages thought not fit to intrust the former two years together. They should be obliged to give an account in public of all their proceedings at the expiration of the said time; and also be under a pecuniary mulct, besides an oath to administer justice impartially, in imitation of God; who to mind them of their great duty, graces them with his own title, saying " Ye are all gods," and therefore must do as I do; you shall not regard " in judgment the power of the mighty, nor the distress of the poor." The judges, lawyers, attorneys and clerks should have out of the public revenue sufficient established salaries to take no fees or gratuity whatsoever, directly or indirectly,

Courts of Judicature.

it not feeming reafonable that the people fhould pay anything for juftice, but as that charge may be included in the public taxes. Let no offices whatfoever be fold, and nothing but merit to entitle any man; for if offices be purchafed by the intereft of friends or money, it is unreafonable to expect that juftice too may not be bought and fold; and for this reafon, it is as fit to make laws againft this practice in others as againft fimony in the clergy. No man fhould have two offices, or act by deputy, but on extraordinary occafions. Let all caufes be determined, at fartheft in fix months; and, as to fuch as through difficulty, or other accidents, cannot be determined within that time, the Parliament at next feffions fhould decide them. Oblige the judges to proceed exactly according to the ftrict rules of the law made by Parliaments: for notwithftanding what the Lord Coke fays, It is their duty only *legem dicere*, not *legem dare;* and therefore, wherever any thing comes to be difputed, of the meaning of the ftatutes, or when any caufe

Courts of Judicature. 65

happens, for which there is not exact and sufficient provision made, they are to have recourse to the Parliament, whose power is not only *legem dare*, but *dicere*. For it appears that in ancient times, when justice was more speedy, and statutes fewer, or rather none at all, the great business of the Parliament was to give sentence in all difficult causes; and to correct the miscarriages, or sinister practice of all inferior courts and officers, and therefore was commonly known by the name of *Curia Magna*. Before the Conqueror's time there was no such thing as courts at Westminster Hall; and the manner then of distributing justice was both speedy and cheap. The county being divided into several portions, there was in every manor a court, where all the causes arising within that precinct were determined by the thane and his assistants; but if too hard, they were removed by appeal to the higher court of the hundred, where all the chief and wise men within that territory with the hundreder or aldermannus gave judgment. If any cause proved too difficult

F

Courts of Judicature.

for this court, then they appealed to the county court, where all the feveral thanes and hundreders, with the chief of the county, called Comes, and fometimes Vicecomes, judged it; but fuch caufes as were too intricate for them were removed to the great court or Parliament, then known by feveral other names; which jurifdiction was exercifed fome ages after the Conqueft; whence Sir Edward Coke may be well fufpected a greater lawyer than an antiquary, or elfe the liberty they took was the occafion of his exalting the judge's power in expounding ftatutes above that of the Parliament.

Having now made it plain that the Parliament has this power, and always had, it were to be wifhed they would make ufe of it, in ftrictly regulating the diforders of all inferior courts, as well ecclefiaftical as civil. This perhaps can never be better done, than after the manner of the famous Venetian commonwealth, by erecting a new magiftracy or court of infpection, public cenfors, men of great candour and integrity, whofe power fhould

Courts of Judicature.

extend to the cognizance of all manner of actions in courts, great and small; and of the demeanour of all officers of the state, of what degree or quality soever. These censors, taking care of the execution of the laws, should be obliged from time to time to give a full and impartial information to the Parliament, in whose power alone it should be, upon conviction of the criminal, to suspend, degrade, or otherwise punish according to the provisions they themselves make in such cases. It should be lawful for all persons to address themselves immediately to these censors, whose information shall by them be fully examined, and neither their informers nor themselves liable to any actions or suits upon account of their proceedings. They should be accountable to the grand and supreme court of judicature; and their number be such as may serve to go circuits round the kingdom. These, as the other judges, to be altered every three years.

And because nothing does more conduce to the good of mankind, next to wholesome

Courts of Judicature.

laws and the practice of piety, than the knowledge of things paſt; not anything being truer than that What is has been, and There's nothing new under the ſun, a perfect relation of which begets a great underſtanding and deep judgment, the ſenſe whereof made a wiſe king ſay, " None were ſo faithful counſellors as the dead;" therefore the Parliament ſhould appoint two of the moſt learned of thoſe cenſors (acquainted with all the moſt ſecret affairs of ſtate, which if not as counſellors, yet as hearers, under the ſame obligation of ſecrecy as ſecretaries or clerks of the council, they may underſtand) to write eſpecially the matters of fact of all affairs and occurrences; the annals not to be made public till the writers and all concerned are gone off the ſtage. The fear of offending and the advantage of flattery being removed, future ages would in the truth of hiſtory find that great rule of judgment and prudence the world has hitherto been deprived of,—there being (a man may ſafely ſay) no true profane hiſtory in the world, ſave that of the wiſe Chineſe, who have obferved this practice for feveral thoufands of years; keeping the records as an arcanum for their princes, who by thefe means have gained a fteady judgment in their own ftate affairs, which is the reafon given for the long and profperous continuance of that great monarchy.

Chapter VIII.

OF LIBERTY, PROPERTY, AND RELIGION.

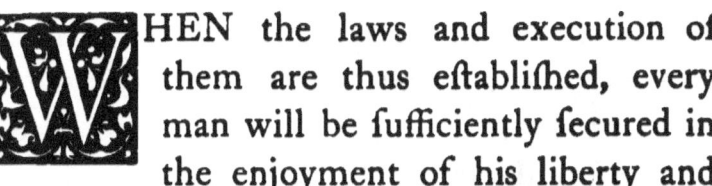HEN the laws and execution of them are thus eftablifhed, every man will be fufficiently fecured in the enjoyment of his liberty and property; which, though commonly taken for two, are in reality one and the fame thing. I underftand by the firft, that power man referved to himfelf when he entered into fociety; that is, a liberty of doing any thing except what the law forbids, or of living conformably to the laws, not of fpeaking contemptuoufly of the rulers of the people, nor of doing what he pleafe though the law reftrain it. By property I conceive is meant the right of enjoying peaceably private poffeffions as bounded by law. Liberty then

respects the person, and property the estate. These two, I perceive, you have joined with religion, as the three great abstracts of human concerns; for I presume you consider religion, as it is, part of that policy by which the state is governed, and as such I shall chiefly take notice of it; leaving it, as it refers to the soul and a future life, to divines, whose proper office it is. Taking it then for granted that every wise man will study that which nearest concerns him, and that the interest of the soul and eternal life does far exceed the value of this our transitory being; that all human laws are therefore binding, because agreeable to nature or reason, that is, to the signatures of the divine will; that true religion was the law of God, and its end the happiness of man in this life, as well as in that which is to come; that it was divided into two parts, duty to God and to one another, which latter to the thinking man, resolves into love of himself,—he must find that his happiness, consisting in the enjoyment of himself, cannot be without the mutual offices and endearments of love, which obliges him, in fpite of all his paffions, when he fully confiders things, to do to all men as he would be done unto. This then, being human happinefs and the end and foundation of the laws of God and man, it was wifdom to annex this great motive of obedience,—religion or the confideration of future rewards and punifhments,—to invite us the more powerfully to the obedience of laws, without which, even in this life, we could not be happy, they being fubordinate to one another. Thus as our duty in one makes us happy here, fo that of the other fuperadds a further bleffing and makes us happy hereafter, which latter in the connection of things thus ordered by Providence was not attainable without the other; and which indeed does declare religion not to be a part of policy, but true policy to be a part of it; or, in plainer words, that human laws are fo much better, that is, fo much more binding, as they come nearer to the laws of religion; contrary to which nothing in any human inftitution can be obligatory; that is, no fociety of men can make that juft which the law of religion or reafon has made unjuft. If then the intereft of ftate and religion be fo intermixed, it is no wonder that men fhould be very folicitous not to be miftaken in that which comprehends both the human and the divine, or among us the Chriftian law. And becaufe it is as natural for men to have different underftandings, confequently different opinions (which are the neceffary effects of the former or of education, and both equally out of our power) as it is to have different complexions, it is impoffible that all men fhould exactly agree in the meaning of any difficult matter. If then the meaning of the law be not to be had, it is not our fault if we do not obey it, which we muft do or be miferable. Now, becaufe many evil confequences, if not prevented, would iffue from hence, we muft confider farther that all wife lawgivers impofe nothing beyond the power of the perfon under the law; for law being the rule of actions, if I do not nor cannot know it, it is no rule to me. Therefore, to understand this great affair aright, let us examine whether thefe following pofitions and their confequences be not natural truths. —Namely, God did really purpofe the happinefs of all mankind; therefore, the way or means by which that was to be attained was to be plain and eafy, no matter of doubt or difpute; and this way is no where delivered unerringly but in the Scriptures, which all Chriftians allow to be the Word of God. Then all the difputes being pretended to be proved by Scripture, that is, by confequences from thence, and all the parts of that holy writing agreeing with one another, it is plain that the confequences are not natural, becaufe contradictory, of which both parts cannot be true, and therefore the matter in difpute concerns us not. Again, fince all our duty is comprifed in Scripture,—the rule for the ignorant as well as the learned, comments do amufe and confound rather than expound the text; and difputes begetting heat and paffion are not only impertinent to our duty, but uncharitable and deftructive of Chriftianity; therefore only the fundamentals can be true or neceffary, becaufe in them alone all agree. Finally, Chrift has told us, the fum of all is, To love one another, a pleafing and a natural command;—that He is the Way, the Truth, and the Life—that whofoever believeth in Him fhall never perifh;—that happinefs is not attainable here nor hereafter but by following His example and believing His doctrine, *viz.* what is pofitively affirmed in Scripture, without examining how or why. If thofe had been neceffary, He would not have left them to the uncertain difputes of after-ages; whilft all ceremonies are in themfelves indifferent, but when commanded are neceffary in their ufe and practice, but alterable at the pleafure of the impofers. No man is a Chriftian that hates his brother, *i. e.* he obeys not Chrift's command, gives not up himfelf to the new commandment, that of loving one another. Moreover, no man can avoid differences in opinion; and fince they are not the effects of our choice, they are not finful; therefore, he that

Liberty, Property,

condemns another for not being of his opinion, after he has endeavoured without prejudice or interest to examine and hold fast that which is best, considers not what he says, or if he do, he is proud and foolish, because he says, by an implicit consequence, none is wise but himself. Faith is the gift of God, but considered in man, it is a necessary act; for when a man is convinced, that is, has no doubts of the credibility of the proposition, its conformity to reason, nor of the person that he can neither deceive, as having no interest, nor be deceived, as wanting no knowledge, it is impossible for him not to give up his assent: whether morality or Christianity be (which is much doubted) really different, they can never be asunder; for the man that is not honest, is not, nor cannot be if he continues so, a Christian. So, what is true in philosophy cannot be false in divinity; and both affirm, he that does all he can do, is not to be blamed, he has done his duty; and different opinions not being avoidable, are in themselves as harmless and tolerable in a society as men can be; because, till the man be convinced, his sense of things cannot possibly be altered: after conviction he that continues in an error, *i. e.* that perseveres in spreading such opinions as are destructive of good life and of public peace, is a liar or a madman; the first, if he do not repent, ought to be expelled the Commonwealth; the other, if he will not grow sober, must be sent to Bedlam. From all which it plainly follows that our opinions are not free, that no man has liberty of opinion, and that he who desires liberty of speaking what he pleases, is unreasonable if he intends to say any thing that shall disturb the peace and quiet of his country; if he may be restrained from that, his errors can mischief no other than himself. If the case then be thus, how comes it to pass, that men fall out and wrangle about nothing, seek knots in bulrushes, make difficulties where God and nature never made any, puzzle themselves and others? Let them fool on that have nothing else to do, and follow the heathen's advice, 'Tis better to do nothing than be idle. This, I confess, would not be very tragical, if they would be content to be idle themselves, and not make work, and sad work too, for others. But, alas! they rob their master of his power, and dogmatically pronounce we must believe more than Christ tells us is required, or else we cannot be saved in the next life, nor happy in this; and many of us are such silly fools that we believe them, and acting accordingly, too great a number, I fear, make their assertions good, as those ignorant people do who, giving credit to astrologers by squaring their actions to the predictions, and therefore sometimes finding these things come to pass, are not only deluded themselves, but encourage others to be so by such nonsensical impostors. But since all men have not understanding, you will ask how the evil shall be cured? The remedies are only two: first, a right education; and, next, a removal of all interest; for, since the foundations of religion are eternal truths, were men rightly instructed, of which all are capable because all designed for happiness, and men got nothing by lying, we should have as much truth and as little disputing in matters of Christianity as in the mathematical sciences; or, at least, if men designed nothing really but the end of it, eternal happiness—it might be lawful for every man, even in the way which another calls heresy, to worship the God of his fathers; for though one thinks his a clearer or a shorter way than that of another, so long as he still goes on, that is, treads in the paths of a sober and virtuous life, though he may be more dabbled, or longer on the road, what is that to him? He that finds fault may miss his own way by looking towards his brother; his particular duty requires all his care; besides, every man stands or falls to his own master. But you will say it is charity to teach my brother, and not to suffer sin upon him. It is very true, but first, it is not proved that difference in opinion is a sin, but the contrary; next, charity is not expressed in thunder and lightning, sending him headlong to the devil, because he will not be presently, whether he can or no, of your opinion, which, perhaps, is not truer than his own, though your greater confidence affert it; but charity is expreffed by meeknefs, gentlenefs, and love; by inftruction and pity, not by hatred and revilings; nay, not by death, the too-often confequence of differences in opinions, from which confiderations it is plain that it is not reafon or charity that divides us, but intereft and policy. How far it will confift with the fafety of the public to fuffer fuch dangerous caufes of fatal effects as are brought in by thefe clafhes of religionifts, not religion, I leave to the wifdom of the Parliament. Only, to fatisfy that part of your queftion, I will give you fome fhort account how thefe tares have fo fprung up as to choke almoft wholly all the good feed fown. Afterwards you may judge if they may not, now the harveft is come, be cut down, gathered apart, and thrown into the fire.

And furely, if thefe quarrels were only defigned for the good of the foul, (which yet if they were the promoters, muft be men of wrong underftanding or notions, forgetting that faith is the gift of God) they would not hate and damn one another for different, though falfe opinions; nothing can have that effect, but the committal of fins, of which holy Scripture pronounces death the wages or neceffary confequence; but thefe we fee paffed over filently, few being excommunicated for whoredom, adulteries, atheifm and profanenefs; many other crimes are openly committed without punifhment, which, perhaps, was the end of inftituting ecclefiaftical courts.

The great defign of Chriftianity was in a higher and more refined way the fame with that which Hierocles tells us of philofophy, the perfection of human life; therefore, the primitive Chriftians, knowing the end of their doctrine was to make men good, to fill their hearts with purity of intention productive of good works, not to make them wife, (if ftuffing their heads with empty and idle notions may be called fo,) avoided all fuch with great care, preffing only upon men the reformation of their lives by the plainnefs of their precepts and their agreeablenefs to reafon; being well affured the contrary practice could bring forth nothing but endlefs janglings and frivolous difputes, which would at laft not only loofen, but deftroy religion by taking away charity, the bond and cement of that and all perfections. But when the piety of fucceeding ages had endowed the Church with temporalities and with rich poffeffions, the churchmen altered their doctrine with their way of living; for now, (kicking like the calves of Jefferon grown fat,) the former practifed feverity was turned into wantonnefs; the plainnefs of the precepts into intricate niceties. This they judged neceffary; for if, according to the promife, the Gofpel was to be fo plain, *i.e.* fo agreeable to Nature and reafon, that a man might running fee to read, *i.e.* a man that made never fo little ufe of his reafon, that did but keep his eyes open againft the falfe allurements of fenfe, could not but perceive the lines of his duty written in very large and plain characters;

perceiving every man thus enabled to teach his brother, and that miracles were ceased, they found themselves under a necessity to make godliness a mystery, that it might become gain to them in an ill sense, and that they might secure to themselves that veneration and respect which otherwise were now like to fail.

Religion, by this means degenerating from its innocence and simplicity into a trade of policy and subtilty, an art to live by, tent-makers and fishermen became too dull and ignorant; the preaching of Christ crucified was fit only for the witty and the learned. No wonder then that being now so much taken up in refining the cobweb inventions of their heads they wanted leisure to look to their feet, to order their steps aright, and therefore went astray, not only from the precepts of the Gospel, but the imitation of the life of the holy Jesus, which was the greater duty of the two; as the end for which his doctrine, the means, was given. To make themselves the more admired they mixed that with the vain philofophy of the Greeks, efpecially Platonifm, with an addition of many abfurd heathenifh and obfolete Jewifh rites and ceremonies. When the bifhops became princes, the number of candidates increafing fafter than preferments could fall, the ambitious were induced to court them by indirect ways, the pretence of an extraordinary knowledge or piety, to gain the intereft and the favour of great men, and by thofe fteps to mount the fpiritual throne of carnal pride. Thus when Arius failed of a bifhopric, enraged that a lefs learned man fhould deprive him of the mitre, he refolved upon a malicious revenge; and to make himfelf more famous than the crofier could, under pretence of difcovering the falfities crept into religion, he alleged one of the great myfteries to have more of Plato's fancy than of Chrift's truth in it; this motherherefy, by him introduced, brought forth many others, and (which was the greater evil) has been the parent of uncharitable difputes, the certain occafions of much confufion

and Religion. 85

in life and doctrine, of affaffinations and maffacres, of wars and defolations.

The Chriftians now, contrary to Chrift's pofitive command, call no man on earth mafter, *i. e.* If an angel from heaven (much lefs a man), fhould preach any other doctrine to you than I (your only lord and mafter) who am now afcending thither enjoin you to obey, *viz.* to love one another, hearken not to him, for he is a murderer and a liar, a cheat and an impoftor. Neglecting this, and having the perfons of men in honour, they readily embraced their opinions; and changing the name of Chriftians, took up that of the fathers of their fects, as of Arians, &c. Thefe divifions and factions, and the confequent bloody wars, would perfuade us that Chrift came not indeed to fend peace on earth, but a fword; for thefe ring-leaders impofed upon the credulous multitude, that all thofe fuper-induced new-fangled, diabolical inventions, unreafonable whimfies and childifh fopperies, were the great pillars and truths of religion, and therefore to be contended for unto death;

Liberty, Property,

while in the meantime they themselves were conscious that they disputed not for truth but victory, for the sensual gratifications of ambition and vain glory of pride and interest; and, if you will but give yourself leisure to look into the controversies of former heretics, or into those of later date, between the Reformed Church and the Church of Rome, &c. you will find them all on one and the same bottom. The Church of Rome has good reason, as to this world, not to yield to any truth in the point of transubstantiation; of which, certainly, it is enough to believe simply Christ's own words, This is my body, because no more is warranted, and therefore not necessary, and that indeed none of the expositions are free from unanswerable objections, though none appear so opposite to sense and absurd as that of the Romanists and Lutherans: for if this power of working miracles be taken from the priest, it may be thought he has nothing left to make him *jure divino;* which, if allowed, he is quick enough to foresee that other princes may follow the example of Henry the Eighth. Thofe miftaken or wilful apprehenfions have involved the feveral kingdoms of Europe in blood and confufion, inteftine commotions and wars, and will embroil them yet further if the caufes be not removed. This has long been the wifh of fome and the endeavour of others, but by the fuccefs—feeing the difeafe is not cured, but that its venom does daily fpread more and more—we may fafely conclude that difputing is as incompetent a way to refettle the truth of religion as the fword is to propagate it. Every man naturally hates to be accounted a fool or a liar, and therefore, when worfted by the force of arguments (which may be to him unanfwerable, though not convincing), he falls into heat and paffion, which, the other returning with equal warmth, at length both lofe the queftion, and fall from words to blows, from difputing to fighting; and, not fatisfied pedantically (for moft commonly the contention is only about words), to lafh one another, they further make parties and factions. These, hurried on with the fury of a perverse zeal, the effect of ignorance, espouse the quarrel, and pursue the folly and the malice to the fatal destruction of thousands of millions; as if there was no getting to the heavenly Canaan, the new Jerusalem, but by wading, or rather by swimming through a Red Sea of Christian blood; while, in the meantime, the first disputants stand looking on, or like sneaking cowards steal away from the rencounter as soon as they have engaged others more generous, but withal more foolish, than themselves. This England has to its cost experimented; and, it is to be feared, if not timely prevented, will again.

Chapter IX.

OF LIBERTY, PROPERTY AND RELIGION (*continued*).

OTHERS, finding the way of dispute insufficient, believed that the allowance of a toleration to the several contending sects would do the work; and that in truth the denial of it, so far as it might consist with the peace of the Commonwealth, seemed to be a kind of persecution not unequal to that of the heathen emperors in the beginning of Christianity. This opinion being by the ringleaders infused into the peoples' minds, who being apt to pity all in distress, from pity are induced to liking, and from liking to love, they at length espouse the party, and with so much the more violence, by how much the more it is opposed; nothing being more natural than to refist force and covet earnestly those things we are forbid. The confideration of this and his own obfervation, that the more the Christians were put to death the more they increased, made the wife Pliny write to the Emperor Trajan to forbear perfecution; telling him "That shedding Christians' blood was sowing the feed of the Church;" every man's death giving to the multitude a fufficient proof of the truth of his profeffion, and gaining more profelytes than preaching could. By the Emperor's following this good advice the Christians gained their liberty, and he an acceffion to his army; and the great increase of converts was thereby much restrained.

The fenfe of this great prudence, joined with his majesty's great natural clemency, has with good reafon prevailed upon his minifters rarely to execute the feverity of the fanguinary and penal laws upon diffenters; and I am well affured that did they not believe by those ftatutes remaining ftill in force that they are under perfecution or the dread of it, inftead of increasing much within these few years they would certainly have decreased. I am therefore persuaded that toleration with convenient restrictions would lessen the evil and remove most of its inconveniences, though all can never be taken away without another sort of education. And if the Parliament that give it find it hereafter inconvenient, they may alter or annul it how they please. In this toleration all opinions are to be provided against that are destructive of good life, together with the consequences rather than occasions, atheism and irreligion. As the Venetians once excluded, so must we for ever prohibit the Jesuits and other regulars; the number of secular priests and nonconforming ministers or teachers are to be limited, they with their flocks registered, and to be incapable of any office in the Commonwealth, and the teacher to be maintained by themselves, the richest of the congregations to be security for their preachers that they shall preach no sedition nor have private conventicles; that besides the state may send two to

Liberty, Property,

hear all taught; that the use of all controversial catechisms and polemical discourses as well out as in the pulpit under strict penalties be forbid; such things, no less in their natures than their names, signifying and begetting distractions, rebellions, and wars. Though it be as impossible by laws or penalties to alter men's opinions from what either their temper or their education has occasioned, as it is to change their complexions, yet if men pursued nothing but godliness and honesty they would find their differences in opinion are no more hurtful than restrainable; and to make them less so, all names of hatred and division are to be taken away, and the parable of Christ's seamless coat to be really fulfilled again. All, whatever their single opinions be, should be called by no other name than that of Christians; for indeed as such they all agree, that is, in the fundamentals of religion, (as for the disputed things they are already shown not certain, therefore not necessary, consequently to us impertinent, which of the assertions be true,) and only differ by the con-

and Religion. 93

fiderations of pride or intereſt as they are Trinitarians or Antitrinitarians, Arians, Socinians, Papiſts or Proteſtants, Remonſtrants or Antiremonſtrants, Janſeniſts or Moliniſts, Franciſcans or Dominicans, Lutherans or Calviniſts, Preſbyterians or Independants, &c. But for my own part I am of opinion that we ſhall never arrive at the true ſtate of Chriſtianity either by diſputing without toleration, or by toleration with diſputing, *i. e.* we ſhall not come to live righteouſly, ſoberly, and godly, in this preſent world; for diſputing deſtroys all, and toleration alone will not take away thoſe wrong notions with which the preſent age is prepoſſeſſed; though ſome of the prejudices may be leſſened by ſoftneſs and gentleneſs, by love and perſuaſions; this I confeſs will not do in all becauſe all have not underſtanding, and ſuch as want it muſt inevitably run into error; for, whatever the philoſophers diſpute whether the will and the underſtanding be diſtinct faculties or diſtinct operations of the ſame ſoul, it plainly appears in all our actions that we will or nil things according to our understandings, which, as well or ill informed, make us do things good or evil; so that, till our notions are rectified, we are to be pitied and instructed, not hated or condemned. When by an excellent education and a good example we are taught not only to know but to practise our duty, it will then be almost morally impossible for us to offend; whereas, on the contrary, while both are now neglected, it is a wonder we are not worse. Pursuant to this, Solomon gives a wise direction, "Train up a child in the way thou wouldst have him to go, and when he is old he will not depart from it." The great business, then, not only to assuage the pain, (which in the present circumstances cannot be done with toleration,) but wholly to remove the distemper, is to introduce such a fixed method of education as may imprint on our minds true and early notions of virtue and religion.

The Parliament have lately begun to look into the practice of piety, and, to prevent or lessen profanation and debaucheries, have en-

and Religion.

acted that hackney coaches (it had been more equal if all had been under the penalty) shall after the Jewish manner of Sabbath, rest from labour; I wish they would now be pleased to take care the people keep the Christian Sabbath as they ought; not so much in a rest from bodily labour as from sin, the greater toil of the soul, to which they are obliged by every day's duty. The use of the seventh, above the rest, seeming to be set apart for returning thanks for blessings and for exhortations effective of holiness and a good life. The duty of that day is not fulfilled by hearing a quaint man preach himself, not Christ; policy, not morality; confute the Pope, the Calvinist, or the Arminian, the Presbyterian or the Episcopal. Such discourses engender nothing but strife, and tend not to edification; they are the vain traditions of men, in which we should quickly find, did we but seriously consider, that there was nothing of that faith without which we cannot please, nor of that holiness without which no man shall see God.

CHAPTER X.

OF LIBERTY, PROPERTY, AND

RELIGION (*continued*).

AND fince the Parliament by that laft mentioned Act have begun to tythe mint, and cummin, it is to be hoped they will go on and not leave the weightier things of the law undone; that their wifdoms and their zeal will be more employed about the power than the form of godlinefs, which may for ever be eftablifhed by the following method, or fuch other as they fhall think more agreeable, *viz.* to make new divifions of parifhes, which may with more convenience to the people be done than as at prefent they ftand, by limiting every parifh to the compafs of about three miles fquare, and building a church in the central-place, to hold about a thoufand; and to apportion the parifhes in cities, at leaft to the like number of people. This will reduce the parifhes from about ten to a little more than four thoufand. Schools fhould be erected in every parifh, where all the children fhall be inftructed in reading, writing, and the firft elements of arithmetic and geometry, without charge to the parents. Whence to the greater fchools to be erected in the diocefes, counties, hundreds, after the manner of Weftminfter, Eton or Winchefter, fo many of the ripeft and beft capacitated, as fhall fuffice for the fupply of all callings that make learning a trade (as divinity, phyfic, and law), may be yearly elected, to be trained up in the further neceffary parts of learning, and from thence yearly fent to the Univerfities. From the Univerfities, upon all vacancies, fchoolmafters and minifters fhould be chofen; the firft, not under five and twenty years; the later, not under thirty (the age allowed among the Jews for doctors or teachers, and at which our Saviour began to preach); and both, to be Mafters of Arts before the one be licenfed or the other ordained by the bifhop; and none to be ordained before they are fecured of being noble men's chaplains, or elected to parifhes. Let the bifhoprics be alfo divided according to convenience and the number of the parifhes. That the minifters and fchool-mafters be celebats, not under a vow (as in the Church of Rome), but on condition of quitting their benefices upon marriage, and returning to a lay life; for that of the priefts being *jure Divino*, being difputed, is therefore (to fay no more) to our falvation not neceffary to be believed; for, unlefs they demonftrate the contrary by Scripture, the fufficient rule of faith, or by miracles, men will be apt to believe the ftory of an indelible character, to be a relic of popery, invented to aggrandize the honour and power of the Church, turned into a court of Rome. But be it what it will, it is plain they cannot be greater than St. Paul, who did not only for convenience of the Church, avoid leading about a wife or a fifter, but wrought at his trade after he had received the Holy Ghoſt; of which it were to be wiſhed all divines ſhewed themſelves poſſeſt, by a life conformable to that of the holy Jeſus. But, without doubt, there will be enough found to undertake this calling on theſe terms, though ſeemingly difficult.

By this courſe there is a proviſion made for the incontinency of ſuch of the prieſts as find themſelves fleſh and blood; which, if done in the Church of Rome, would free it from great ſcandal.

Let a book of homilies be compiled; for variety four every Sunday, and two for each feſtival or holy day. Let nothing be inſerted but dehortations from vice and exhortations to virtue, neither controverſies nor ſtate affairs ſo much as obliquely glanced upon. Let a catechiſm, adapted to the meaneſt capacity, be compoſed, ſhewing the duty of Chriſtians according to the expreſs words of the text of Scripture, without ſtraining or miſapplying any one, (as is done in too many of thoſe now extant), and without touching upon any one diſputed point. All the books of controverſial Divinity, as well thoſe in private hands as in bookſellers, ſhould be bought up by the ſtate, and placed in the King's Library or burnt. All the Commentaries on the Bible ſhould be reviewed by ſober, moderate, and learned men; and as many of them as contain more than what directly tends to the illuſtration of the text, by recounting the language, cuſtoms, and ceremonies of the times and places it was writ in, follow the fate of the others. And becauſe it is reaſonable to believe there is no ſuch entire work extant, in imitation of the Septuagint tranſlation, there may be ſeventy appointed for this to be in Latin, and for the Homilies and Catechiſm in Engliſh; which being done, let all the preſent expoſitions be ſent to the library or the fire. Let the ſame perſons or others be ordered to pick out of the Scripture all ſuch paſſages as tend to the encouragement of a holy life, and to put them into one piece in Engliſh for common uſe.

I have heard ſome ſober men wiſh that

Englifh bibles were not fo common that the ignorant and unwary might not wreft the hard texts to their own deftruction, nor to that of the public peace: but you know I have often told you I looked upon the variety of tranflations out of the original into the vulgar languages as the beft comment.

Chapter XI.

OF LIBERTY, PROPERTY, AND RELIGION (*continued*).

THESE things being done, to take the printing of books into the ſtate, it is as neceſſary as the Mint. Falſe coinage of books having done England more miſchief than ever that of money did, or will do, the licenſing of printing, or importing from beyond ſea, will not otherwiſe prevent great evil to Church and State. Let there be but a convenient number of bookſellers permitted; thoſe to be under obligation to vend no other books than ſuch as are printed in this allowed printing-houſe, where foreign books, with advantage to the public, may be reprinted. The hindering foreign coin from being current is not ſo uſeful and advantageous, as the care in this will prove, to the kingdom.

When things are thus far settled, the bishops (who are not to be chosen under forty) are to see that all ministers, schoolmasters and churchwardens, do their respective duties; going about, and visiting parish by parish, as was the ancient practice; confirming after examination, and exhorting all to continue obedient to the laws of God and man; reprehending and suspending such as they find faulty without favour or affection, the ministers and schoolmasters from office and benefice; the people from the sacrament (which is everywhere monthly at least, to be administered) till after repentance expressed in the reformation of their lives.

As for the jurisdiction of ecclesiastical courts, because it is a kind of *imperium in imperio*, and that through the greatness of the bishops' other charge, they cannot officiate in this to take away and prevent abuses, it is to be laid aside; and other, or the same punishments for the crimes there usually tryable, inflicted in the ordinary courts, upon the bishops' or the minister and church-wardens'

Liberty, Property,

certificate of the matter of fact; in whom alone the power of examination should reside. And, becaufe the office of bifhops, minifters and fchool-mafters will be of great labour, none fhould continue in them beyond fixty, nor fo long unlefs they are found fitting: after that age, all of them to have a handfome decent retreat in colleges purpofely built; where the fuperannuated of each province, the *emeriti* in the Chriftian warfare, may fpend the remnant of their days, without care, in quiet and devotion.

To affift and eafe the bifhop, there fhould be as formerly, rural deans over every ten or twenty parifhes. Part of the minifter's bufinefs fhould be to inftruct the boys, every Saturday in the fchools, in all the duties of religion; to catechife and read the prayers and homilies on Sundays in public; the reft of the week, between the times of prayer to be celebrated twice a-day, to go from houfe to houfe, exhorting and dehorting, as occafion requires, vifiting the fick, and examining the needs of the poor, reconciling

and Religion.

differences between the neighbours, and taking care that in every family the children, such as are found fit by the electors appointed, not by the parents' blind fondness, be constantly sent to school.

After the continued practice of this course, Christianity will again flourish; the years of the minister will make him sober and grave, fit to give counsel, which from young men is now despised. There will then be no need of spending time in writing controversies or studying sermons, which, as now preached, are rarely understandable or useful to the people; of whom it may be said, the one is always teaching to no purpose, and the other ever learning, and never coming to the knowledge of the truth.

The schoolmasters are not only to be learned, but sober and discreet men; to be obliged never to whip, or beat the boys; whose faults are to be punished by exercises, by standing mute, or kneeling for certain spaces, or by fasting from their victuals, &c. Those that are good, to be encouraged by priority of places, by commendatory verses made by the higher forms, &c. The boys that need beating, are as unfit to be taught, as the man is to teach who uses that tyrannical way, which too much debases the meek-spirited, and makes the sullen more stubborn and ill-natured. Let whatever any persons bestow on the masters be converted to public charitable uses. The method of teaching should be drawn up by some of the members, (who, it is presumed, will mix things with words), and approved by the whole of the Royal Society. Let that be confirmed and all others prohibited by law.

In the Universities, none should be suffered to continue beyond the age of forty-five, nor above two in any one house or college after thirty-five. Let a new method be likewise framed by the same persons for all the liberal arts and sciences; and let new academies be built for training up young noblemen and gentlemen in those exercises which, to the shame and loss of England, are now learnt in France.

and Religion. 107

Handsome and sufficient salaries should be fixt, and paid out of the public revenue, according to every man's quality: bishops equal to one another, deans to deans, ministers and school-masters to each other; and these to be chosen gradually, as the pure consideration of merit shall invite the electors. And to enable the public as well in paying these salaries, as in building of schools, churches, colleges and hospitals, the whole revenues of the church, free-schools, universities and hospitals should at the highest value be annexed to the crown, or sold to others that will give more. The overplus saved by this new model, and the money they would yield beyond any other land of England, in regard the annual rent is not a fourth of the real value, and yet may be ordered equally advantageous to the tenants, as the fines now make them, would complete this work. Thus converting the patrimony of the church would be no sacrilege, the pious use is carried on to the good of all; and perhaps as first designed by the

Liberty, Property,

donors, when provifion for wives and children not in being could not be thought of; the care of whom diftract many from their duty, and difable them from keeping in decent repair the ancient monuments of piety built by our anceftors. But all thefe things fhould be done without the leaft prejudice to the prefent incumbents.

When education is thus fettled, the duty and intereft of church-men and their care of wives and children removed, plurality of livings and fimony prevented, as well that of friendfhip, of the fmock, marrying of coufins, nieces, crooked fifters or ladies' women, as that of the purfe, (all which in themfelves are equally criminous,) none but good men will undertake the charge. Then the objections will vanifh which loofe education has infufed into the wild and foolifh, viz. That religion is a cheat, a trick of ftate; that the parfon follows Chrift for the loaves; fpeaks as does the lawyer in his trade, not that there is any truth in it, but becaufe he has *bos in lingua*, &c. To do this is neither fo ftrange nor so difficult as was the greater alteration made by Henry the Eighth, who had not in story been so infamous, though he had seized on the whole temporalities of the Church, had he but thus disposed of some part. And by the way you may take notice, that the House of Commons in this point had been Cromwells in the sixth and eleventh years of Henry the Fourth, who upon their advice would have seized the Church's patrimony, had they not by friends and money prevented the blow; and that *de facto*, several bishoprics and livings were enjoyed by some of his predecessors, which appears not only from history, but from printed acts of parliament.

It will be no hard matter, from Grant's observations and the bills of mortality, to make a computation of the numbers necessary to be sent yearly to the Universities for divinity, law, and physic; the last of which ought so to be regulated as not to suffer any to kill, rather than cure, which is daily done in London and other parts of the kingdom, to the prejudice and scandal of that honourable and sometimes useful profession, to the loss of the people's money and lives, to the maintaining of many idle and ignorant mountebanks and impostors, who, to the greater advantage of the Commonwealth, might be employed in more safe and beneficial trades or ways of living.

This course will also prevent such evil consequences in Church and State as formerly attended the superfœtations of the clergy, and the breeding up of servitors and poor scholars (as they well call them) in the Universities. They are generally of mean birth, and no less mean parts, and the attendance upon their masters does not suffer them so well to attend their studies; so their subsistence by service failing them after they had stayed at the University no longer than to incapacitate and unfit them for any other way of living, and yet not to qualify them for turning preachers; however, having chopped a little logic and disputed of *ens rationis*, and so fancying they could build castles in the air, they assume the confidence to conclude they

and Religion.

cannot mifs of habitations on the earth. Hence from the loweft of the people, getting to be put into the prieft's office for a piece of bread, they become a great caufe of, as well as they are in effect, the contempt of the clergy. Thefe men, for want of knowledge, lay their foundations in erroneous doctrines, in which, neverthelefs, they could not fucceed, but by pretending an extraordinary meafure of faintfhip or holinefs, railing at the fins and abufes of the times, which themfelves have occafioned. Thus they creep into houfes, and firft lead filly women, and then their hufbands captive, as Adam by Eve's perfuafion eating the forbidden fruit till he furfeited and died; fo thefe ignorant zealots, not content in King James's time and the beginning of King Charles the Firft, to rob the kingdom of many families, made themfelves the *boute-feus* of the late horrid rebellion. Though indeed it may be faid to have been principally occafioned by fuch as thefe, yet it was not without fome epifcopal men having a finger in the pie: for, to fay truth,

Liberty, Property,

I know not whether the too great ftiffnefs in the one for their old, or in the other, againft the new forms was moft blameable. But this I know, that by the collifion of both parties, as of flints, a fire was kindled not unlike that in the tails of Samfon's foxes, which proved as deftructive of the expectations of profit each had of their own crop as the other did to the Philiftines' corn; yet had the evil of that not extended to any others but thofe of the pulpit, we might now have talked of it without much regret. Whatever fuch violent difputes have formerly been able to do, it is my duty to wifh, and yours to endeavour, that England be no more the ftage of fuch tragedies. Refrain not counfel when it may do good, and be not backward in advifing that TOLERATION is the firft ftep and EDUCATION the next that perfectly leads the way to peace and happinefs. This courfe being taken, we fhall have no caufe to defpair but that religion will again refume its naked truth, that the doctrines of men will be judged better or worfe as they more or less incline to holiness of living; and thus, being reduced to a calmness within ourselves, we need not fear the designs of foreigners.

CHAPTER XII.

THE INTEREST OF ENGLAND IN REFERENCE TO FRANCE.

OF foreigners none but France can be fuppofed to have any defigns upon England; and if that be granted, why may it not be prevented by obferving ftill the fame rules of policy which this crown formerly practifed; that was, fo holding the balance between the then two contending powers of Spain and France, that neither fhould be able to obtain their aims—the univerfal monarchy of the weft? But now the cafe is altered, in that Spain being much weakened by the acceffion of the Weft Indies, and grafping more than it could well hold in other countries, has quitted the field and left France without a rival; fo that the prefent intereft of England feems to be the fame

in reference to France.

with that of all Europe, viz. to oppofe by all poffible means the growing greatnefs of France; and reduce that crown to fuch a condition as may not leave it in his power to hurt his neighbours. By what they have already compaffed one may guefs they will ere long bring about, if not timely ftopped, their long-defigned ambitious purpofes; in the profecution of which they were in the late times of ufurpation, the underhand inftrument of the war with Holland, as they were of the two following in 1665 and 1671, blowing up the feuds on both fides, pretending to take part with each, but not really purpofing it with either. Having the fame defign of weakening both parties, as the Britons formerly had in throwing a bone of contention between the Picts and Scots, that they might in the end be the better able to overcome both. In the mean time the French king gained an opportunity of building fhips of war, and training up feamen, of which he was before deftitute; fo that had not thefe quarrels and our late civil wars given him a pretence of increasing his maritime power, we might still, even by threats of burning the ships upon the stocks or in the harbours, as did Queen Elizabeth, have kept that people under and ourselves from fear; but since, by unavoidable accidents, the dice are so thrown as that the fore is lost, let us use the best of our art and skill to retrieve an after-game. There is no need to attempt the proof of what is as evident as the sun at noon-day, that the French king has a power great enough, considering the present circumstances of Europe, to make him hope, and all others dread his effecting that old design, which has been the end of all actions of that crown for many years past. Before he could put his design in execution, his great obstacle and rival the Spaniard was to be removed out of the way; in order to which he judged necessary to fortify himself with some allies, and engage others neuters; but foreseeing it was the interest of England and Holland to oppose the one and assist the other, and therefore despairing to prevail

in reference to France.

upon either, he contrived to make both fall out. Not long after he took the advantage of unexpectedly invading the Spaniſh Netherlands, even while his agent, then in Spain, was perſuading that crown of his maſter's good intentions to continue in entire peace and amity with them. The conſequence of which we wiſely foreſeeing, occaſioned our ſetting on foot the Triple League in the year 1668, by which a ſtop was put to his further progreſs.

And now perceiving himſelf diſappointed, he makes various attempts in the years 1669 and 1670 to invite England to break that alliance; but finding his fineſſe vain, he obliquely endeavours it, by renewing the old, and inventing new grounds of quarrels, by ſuch agents and penſioners in the ſtate of Holland as his wealth had purchaſed. This at laſt made them commit ſuch inſolence againſt the honour of this crown, and the intereſt of the people in point of trade, as brought upon them the laſt fatal war, into which he no ſooner drew the Hollanders,

The Intereſt of England

than he ruſhed into the very heart of their country. This ſudden event made them confeſs their error, and our king the ſooner to conclude a peace. The Parliament was then and ſince very deſirous his majeſty ſhould engage with the Dutch and Spaniards againſt France; and without doubt he knew it would be his intereſt ſo to do, but not at that time. For though the undoubted prerogative of the kings of England entitles them to make war and peace, he did not waive the former becauſe the Parliament urged it, as the malicious ſuggeſt, but becauſe he ſaw it not convenient. It is true, the kings of England have been pleaſed to adviſe in ſuch matters with their Parliaments, but that was an act of grace and condeſcenſion, and ought not now (if at all) to be inſiſted on, ſo as to deny the king that liberty which, as a man he cannot want, that of examining and approving or diſapproving what his great council ſhould adviſe. For no man in his wits will dream the Lords and Commons have a power of impoſing what they pleaſe upon the king, when without his assent they have neither power nor right to make any act. The king considered that peace is the happiness of a kingdom; that war being a real evil is never to be undertaken but to avoid a greater; that his treasures were exhausted by the war just finished; that his people had not recovered their losses by the plague, fire, and wars, and therefore were unable to bear the burden of heavy taxes, which of necessity must have been imposed to carry on a new one, for which great preparations ought to be made, both of men, money, and shipping; the former were no less wanting than the last much impaired and diminished. He considered that the French king had not only been amassing great treasure for many, but had also been three years training up an army in all the disciplines of war; that it was necessary before one king entered into a war, to compare his own and the other's strength, " whether with ten he were able to meet him with twenty thousand;" that he ought to make alliances, and to have cautionary towns, before we declared ourselves enemies; that so great a design was not to be made public before things were ripe, left the Dutch and French might clap up a peace, and that potent king turn against us the fury of his arms, for whom certainly in those circumstances we should have been a very unequal match. I am persuaded that these, with other much wiser considerations not obvious to every man, convinced the king a war was on no score at that time seasonable; and to this opinion I am moved, by my sense that the king could not but reflect, that when the French king had subjected all the rest of Europe, he would not fail to add England to his conquests, in which our king's loss must needs be greater than his subjects'. It is unreasonable to think that true policy would let the French king suffer any of the royal family, especially the King of England and France (at whose title and arms-bearing he is not a little offended) to outlive the loss of the crown, since he could not but believe they would be perpetually endeavouring the regaining their own right; for though subjection be uneasy to all, it is not so intolerable to any, as to those used to govern. Therefore it is an idle, senseless and inconsiderate fancy to imagine the king and duke could forget their own interest, or be frenchified upon any promise or bargain, as is maliciously insinuated, that they might be more absolute, which cannot possibly be in their thoughts or wishes who know that between kings or states, covenants are binding no longer than convenient,—that the French king has ever shown that his interest only or his will is the rule of convenience,—that he that makes war for his glory has more ambition to put his chains upon princes than on the people. His thoughts are as large as any of the Roman emperors, and they esteemed it a greater glory to lead one king in triumph, than many thousand subjects of several kingdoms. And it is not to be supposed that the natural strength and situation of England can be a sufficient defence against the power of France,

The Intereſt of England

when to that he has already is added that of all the reſt of Europe, unleſs you can dream they may have a fleet greater than all, and may at once reſiſt, by thoſe walls, the invaſion of others, and defend their merchantmen at ſea, which if not done without an invaſion, by ſpoiling the trade England will be deſtroyed, or which is altogether as bad, be rendered very poor and inconſiderable. And that this has been his majeſty's ſenſe, may be gueſſed by the progreſs he has made ſince the war, mediating a peace as beſt became a good king, and giving his ſubjects an opportunity of enriching themſelves, and enabling them to bear the neceſſary taxes, by engroſſing moſt of the trade of Europe, and at length finding his endeavours ineffective, he prepared himſelf to reſiſt the French deſigns by force, by providing a fleet, and knowing that he that fights with another muſt have ſkill at the ſame weapons, he ſuffered ſuch of his ſubjects as were willing (but on capitulations to return when he pleaſed) to ſerve either the confederates or the French, not only to be fitted to lead others, but also to understand the new arts of fighting, which are greatly altered from what they were in former times. The king having thus prepared things, I hear he is so far from being backward to declare war with France, that he will gladly do it, if his Parliament will but find out a sufficient means for carrying it on effectually: which I apprehend must not be ordinary, for that the war, if undertaken, is like to be of long continuance.

And you will guess that it is no longer to be delayed, if you will but bring before your eyes the danger we and all Europe are exposed to, by comparing the present power of France with what it was in the days of Francis the First, and observing what he was then able to do, when assaulted by Charles the Fifth, who was not only emperor, but had all the power of Spain, of the seventeen provinces, of Naples, Sicily, Sardinia, the dukedom of Milan, and the riches of the West Indies; who was as wise, courageous, and fortunate a captain, as moſt ages of the world have known; one who managed his own councils, and like Alexander in every action appeared at the head of his army; who had above a hundred thouſand well diſciplined men, led by many great and experienced commanders; who was able, by a mighty naval power, to begirt France on both ſides, from Flanders and from Spain. Yet at that time France courting the ſame miſtreſs, the univerſal monarchy, was ſo powerful a rival that he durſt not attempt his removal out of the way of his ambition, without the aid and aſſiſtance of Henry the Eighth, the Pope, and ſeveral princes of Italy; nor even then did he think himſelf ſecure till he had drawn to a defection Charles, Duke of Bourbon, the moſt conſiderable Prince of France. And yet after all he was forced to clap up an accommodation on terms ſufficiently advantageous to that crown.

If ſo mighty a power, and ſo united, could not prevail againſt Francis the Firſt, how unlikely is it to reſiſt Louis the Fourteenth,

in reference to France. 125

a much greater prince, when that power is now fo much leffened by being broken and divided into feveral hands; when the Emperor gives himfelf up more to devotion than martial or ftate affairs; when the king of Spain is a youth of fixteen, and when the feventeen provinces are cantoned between the Spaniard and the States General; when thefe feveral divifions and interefts occafion long debates, different opinions, and flownefs in preparation and action; when all that was formerly managed by one fingle head, is by thefe accidents brought under the conduct of feveral governors, of whom it is poffible fome may prefer their private advantages to the interefts of their mafters. This has made fome conjecture the French king has opened more gates with filver keys than by force of arms; and has induced others to conclude that the Confederates will hardly be able to defend the remainder of the Spanifh Netherlands another campaign, if not affifted by the joint power of the reft of Europe. This you will eafily believe not to

The Intereſt of England

be ill grounded, if you conſider the preſent greatneſs of France: Louis has about four times the revenue Francis had, and at leaſt four times the army; nay, rather, all his people are now in a manner ſoldiers. It is not only ſcandalous, but a vain attempt, for any gentleman there to make court for a wife before he has ſerved a campaign or two, nor are any of the nobleſſe ſuffered to live at eaſe in the country, that do not go or ſend ſome of their ſons to the war. Theſe practices enabled him, laſt ſummer, in fifteen days to ſend forty-five thouſand gentlemen, with their ſervants, at their own charge, to raiſe the ſiege of Charleroy. And to make the monarchy more abſolute, matters have been ſo ordered that their Parliaments are become ordinary courts of juſtice, and have no other laws than the edicts of the prince's will. And if at any time he condeſcends in formality to aſſemble the three eſtates (who had in Francis the Firſt's time the power of Parliaments) it is but to tell them by his chancellor the king wills you do thus or thus; you are not to advife or difpute, but immediately ratify his commands, which accordingly are obeyed, as the effects of a defpotic power.

In the beginning of the year 1665, he was not able to man out twenty fhips of war, and now he has about two hundred; he has not only vaft treafures heaped together, but the ftrings of all the purfes of his flaves, rather than fubjects, in his own hands. If without any affiftance he has already gained Lorraine, Franche Compte, a great part of Flanders, and no inconfiderable footing in Germany and Sicily, and in the beginning of the laft campaign, three fuch ftrongholds as Valenciennes, St. Omer, and Cambray; the weakeft of which, moft men thought, would at leaft have made him a whole fummer's work, what will he not be able to compafs againft the reft of Europe, when he has got the acceffion of Germany and all the Low Countries to that already too boundlefs power by which he has fettered his own people, and fubjected them to an abfolute vaſſalage? Will other nations expect better terms than he has given his own? It is well if he will allow them even canvas and ſabots. But, above all, what can England hope, having for many years forced him to check the reins of his ambition, and being, I preſume, at this time ready to put on the bridle? Books have already been printed ſhowing his pretenſions to this country, which, though weak and ſilly, may help to ſpur him on in the purſuit of his glory. Nor can leſs be expected from thoſe who, by a confederacy with the late uſurpers, gave an opportunity of taking away the life of the firſt Charles, and of purſuing that of the ſecond, to whom his own couſin german inhoſpitably denied the continuance of a retreat, when the viciſſitudes of human affairs, to make him afterwards appear more glorious, veiled him in clouds of misfortunes. What can be hoped from him who contrived that never to be forgotten affront of burning our ſhips at Chatham, and who is ſaid to have had no ſmall hand in the firing of London; who, though styled the most Christian, declares, as an unalterable maxim, no treaty binding longer than it consists with his interest,—not founded on religion or reason, but on glory? The very heathens were anciently and the Turks at this day are more punctual to their oaths and promises,— the falsifying of any thing confirmed by the adjuration of their gods, or Mahomet, was and is accounted infamous. But what treaties or capitulations can be reckoned which the French ministers have not violated? Have they not broken the famous Pyrenean treaty, confirmed by oath and sacraments? And, contrary to a solemn renunciation and the double ties of blood and marriage, before a breach complained of or a war declared, invaded the territories of an infant king? Have not they by address and cunning, by bribes and rewards, endeavoured to corrupt most of the ministers of Europe? Such practices amongst private Christians would be abominable, and much more so between any kings not styled the most Christian. Do they not publicly abet the proceedings of the rebels in Hungary againſt their lawful prince? And whatever the Pope may be induced to believe, not for the propagation of the Romiſh religion (for they are Proteſtants), but to ſerve his own ambitious purpoſes of enſlaving the world; of which, rather than fail, he has decreed to bring in the Turk, in whoſe courts alſo he has found arts to make his coin current. Nor is the infallible man, whom he has already pillared, to eſcape him, at leaſt as to the temporal part of his power; for, not thinking that affront great enough, and concluding he has not, as he ought, employed it for the French intereſt, he is ſaid to have privately vowed not only the leſſening but the abrogating of that great authority in which his predeceſſors Pepin and Charlemagne's charity had veſted him. Nor is his countenancing the Janſeniſts, a ſect more dangerous to the ſee of Rome than that of Luther or Calvin, a ſmall argument that he intends to pull down his ſpiritual grandeur by fixing it in a Gallican patriarch. But, to come nearer home, have not *in reference to France.*

the French had a main hand in our civil wars, and were they not fince the fecret inftruments of fpilling the blood of many thoufands of our fellow fubjects? To fome of whom, though now they pretend civility, it is not to give them a fhare in their glory fo much as to hazard their lives, making them fteps to the throne of an unjuft empire; in order to which they have expofed them on all occafions, in hopes by weakening us to remove out of their way the greateft block which has already given them check, and will now, I hope, ftop their career and mate them. And is it not time, think you, that all the princes in Chriftendom, for their common fafety, fhould unite, not only to chafe the French king out of his new conquefts, but confine him to his ancient dominion and manner of government? If this be not fpeedily put in execution, I may without the fpirit of prophecy foretell fome of the princes of Germany and Italy who now feem unconcerned, will, when it is too late, repent the overfight. The fire is already kindled in their neighbourhood, and if they do not help to quench the flame, they will quickly fee their own dwellings laid in duft and afhes. Every new acquift and acceffion of power enlarges our defires, and makes the ambitious man think that which before feemed not only difficult but impoffible, to be plain and feafible;—the fuccefs of the French has already made them think no enterprife too hard, and ftill prompts them to pufh on their good fortune, which nothing can withftand but a general oppofition of other princes.

You fee then it is not fo much honour nor friendfhip, nor a defire of fuccouring the injured and oppreffed that invites the reft of Europe to the affiftance of the Netherlands, but the care and prefervation of their own laws and liberties, their glory and their fortunes. And though I am apt to believe on England's entering into the league, the French king would gladly conclude a peace, yet I cannot but think the doing fo would be againft the common intereft on any other terms than quitting all his new acquifitions, and even then the confederates will be out in policy if they do not ftill continue in a pofture of defence both by fea and land. The Dutch paid dear for the contrary practice, and their fufferings in 1672 will convince them and others that fo long as Louis the Fourteenth lives, his neighbours muft not expect to fleep in quiet; they cannot prudently hope his future practices will be more juft than his former; he that has already broken through fo many obligations of oaths and treaties is likely to do fo again. Whoever cannot be kept within bounds by the fenfe of reafon and juftice will defpife the weaker ties of forced oaths. For he that avows power to be the rule, and ftrength the law of juftice, will not ftick to fay this peace was an impofition, an unjuft reftraint of the lawful purfuit of his greatnefs. And therefore as foon as he gives his wearied armies a breathing time, and fees the confederates difperfed and their troops difbanded, he will, like an unexpected torrent, break in upon fome of his neighbours. The common infcription of his cannons, *ratio ultima regum*, is by him inverted to a contrary sense, and made a public warning to mankind that he designs, as God did of old, to give law in the world in thunder and lightning, to scatter by the flames of his artillery all those clouds of the confederate forces that intercept and eclipse the rays of his glory. He makes the power of his arms his first and last reason. He does not only pursue but commonly wounds his adversary before he declares him such, or gives him leisure to draw. First invades a prince's territories, and after sets up his title and cause of the war; is not concerned that all the world observes the pretence is false and trifling, vain and unjust, warranted by no other reason than that of absolute and unbounded will, that he will do so because he will; which is the foundation and conclusion of all his actions and wars abroad, as well as of his laws and edicts at home, expressed in these imperious words, *Tel est nostre plaisir*. He does not only tread in the steps, but outgoes one of his predecessors, who in a quarrel with his Holiness, sent him word that what he could not juftify by *canon* law, he would by the law of the *cannon*.

His device, the fun in its meridian, with his motto, *Non pluribus impar*, fufficiently fhows his intentions for the univerfal monarchy, and the haughty opinion he conceives of his being the only perfon qualified for the government of more worlds than one, declares his refolutions of admitting no rivals in fovereignty, looking upon all other princes but as fo many fmaller ftars or wandering planets compared with him, the Sun; from whom after the antiquated and juftly exploded opinion of fome philofophers, they are to receive their borrowed light or power, as it fhall pleafe his mightinefs to difpenfe; fo that crowned heads, princes and republics, as well as their fubjects, are to expect the fame meat, that of flavery; and though that be not fweet, yet the fauce will be four, poignant to all, however, perhaps a little differenced. The former may be allowed golden, while the latter are to be manacled with iron chains.

The Intereſt of England

In order hereunto, his ambition has made him reſolve the conquering of the world after the example of Alexander, whoſe title of Great, as an earneſt of his future hopes, he has already aſſumed. He has vowed to make himſelf as famous to poſterity by his ſword, though not by his pen, as Cæſar has done; that Paris ſhall give law to the univerſe as Rome once did, and that the Ocean ſhall yield no leſs to the Seine, than formerly it did to Tiber. Now if England, which alone is able to do it, prevents the execution of theſe vaſt purpoſes, what can we expect but that one time or other he will ſeek a revenge, and, notwithſtanding his promiſes and ſolemn confirmations of peace, try againſt us the ſucceſs of his arms, and by numbers endeavour for this mighty inſolence to chaſtiſe thoſe for whom even their own hiſtories will convince them, they are man to man a very unequal match.

The diſbanding his forces for the preſent is far from being a ſecurity, ſince he may raiſe them again at his pleaſure. Nor indeed do I imagine he will difcharge his armies, fince that were to give them an opportunity of rebelling, for which he is fenfible his people are fufficiently prepared, and only want either domeftic heads and partifans, or foreign affiftance, to refcue themfelves from tyranny and oppreffion. And is it fit, while fo potent and fo near a monarch is in arms that we fhould ftand with our hands in our pockets? No, I am perfuaded, though a prefent peace fhould be concluded, that the king and his minifters will think it for the common fafety and the particular intereft of England, not only to enter with the confederates into a ftrict alliance offenfive and defenfive, but alfo to put themfelves into a pofture of war both at fea and land. The end of war is peace, but a peace with France feems to me to be the beginning of war, or, at leaft, a preparation for one; and I muft ingenuoufly profefs, though war be a great evil, yet from all appearances, I dread the confequences of a peace more for that without great care it will be of the two the moft fatal to England. But this confideration, as moft fit, I leave to my fuperiors, and will only afk you, whether before we engage in a war abroad, it be not fit to fecure a peace at home; to reconcile by toleration our differences in point of religion, that the French emiffaries, or others, may not be able to ftrike fire into the tinder already prepared for the leaft fpark. It muft not be forgotten that, to divert or difable Queen Elizabeth from affifting France or defending Holland, Philip the Second of Spain encouraged and affifted Tyrone to rebel in Ireland; that in the long war between us and France, it was the frequent practice of that crown to incite the Scots to make incurfions upon us; and I prefume, it will be confidered, whether fome ambitious men of that kingdom may not influence the people to favour or fide with a prince who maintains great numbers of their nation, by the confiderations that they are now but a province; that England denies them an equal freedom in traffic; that they may have better terms from the French in

in reference to France. 139

that and religion, in which by denial of liberty they seem dissatisfied.

Though such persons cannot possibly work on the wise, the considerative of the people, yet sure it were not improper to study a course to prevent the unthinking crowd, the rabble's being deluded by such false and groundless pretensions; which in my opinion are with more care to be provided against in Ireland, where it is said those and other motives may be urged; for there are computed to be in that kingdom about eleven hundred thousand persons, of which 800,000 are Irish, and of them above 10,000 born to estates, dispossessed. These for their losses, and others for restraint in matters of religion, are discontented, not considering their own rebellion occasioned their ruin: (by their murmurings I perceive, let the sentence be never so just, it will not hinder the condemned from railing against the judge:) Besides their suffering in estate and religion, they are yet further, beyond the Scots, rendered incapable of enjoying any office or

The Intereſt of England

power military or civil either in their native or any other of their prince's countries; their folly having thus reduced them to a condition more like that of ſlaves than ſubjects. Many of the gentry go frequently into other kingdoms, but moſt into France, who may poſſibly be encouraged to return to move the people to a new ſedition, eſpecially if they can give them aſſurance of foreign aſſiſtance. The king wifely foreſeeing this, directed, in 1673, his late vigilant and prudent vicegerent, the Earl of Eſſex, to diſarm the Iriſh papiſts, and notwithſtanding the exact execution of that command, it is ſaid that his majeſty intends to put himſelf to the further charge of increaſing his army in that kingdom beyond what now it is, and to appoint a conſiderable ſquadron of ſhips to guard and defend its coaſts from any attempts of invaſion, without which there is not the leaſt fear of any inteſtine commotions.

This, with the charge he has been at in erecting a new fort in the harbour of Kinſale, the moſt likely place to prevent the entering of any foreign power into that country, shows he has been watchful to secure himself and people against the French designs. And now I touch upon Ireland, I have heard some say that it is not only convenient but necessary to unite that kingdom to this, to make a new division of shires, to send only so many members to Parliament as could no more join to outvote us than Cornwall and Devonshire with two or three other counties; and I see not if they were thus made one wherein their interest would be different from ours, although many rather think they would be losers by the bargain. Others fancy Poyning's act should be repealed, that at first, though a trick, it was necessary but now is not, all the power and almost all the land being devolved upon such as are mediately or immediately English and Protestants. Thus by an easy contrivance they might be still obliged to a dependence on the crown of England; by which, it is said, if they are always so kept under as to be no more than hewers of wood and drawers of water, they may in future ages

The Interest of England

be encouraged to a defection, and either set up a power of their own, or invite a foreigner, which might prove of ill consequence to England; for the harbours and situation of Ireland lying more convenient for trade, makes it that way or otherwise a ready inlet to the conquest of England.

The people there stomach the prejudice in point of commerce, designed though not effected, by the acts against their cattle, navigation and plantation trade; by the first they are said to have gained vastly by an increase in woollen and linen manufactures, in shipping and foreign traffic, to the great prejudice of England. And I have been credibly informed by a person who examined it, that they have gained, *communibus annis*, 40,000*l.* sterling yearly by the exported commodities of beef, tallow, hides, butter, and wool yielding so much more after the passing that act than they and the cattle did before when transported together. And if the Irish, of which there are few pure families left, have some pretence to the king's favour, as he is lineally descended from Fer-

gutius, second son of the then reigning king
of Ireland, and first of Scotland, which was
anciently peopled from thence; the English
there claim a greater share in his majesty's
grace, and say of right they ought to be
accounted but the younger brothers of England.
I could wish with all my heart the
story were true I had from an Irish gentleman
in France, that his countrymen were so
pleased that they were at last governed by a
king descended from their own blood royal,
that they had resolved to pay his majesty and
the successors of his line the allegiance due
from natural born subjects, not from a conquered
people, which they now no more
esteem themselves, nor desire to be accounted
by others. How much of this may be true,
you and I know not, but this I think, if all
the natives were obliged to speak English, and
all called by the name of the English of Ireland,
and allowed equal privileges in trade,
(the same usages and customs, begetting a
harmony in humour,) that rancour might in
time be removed, which from a sense of being

conquered renders them now troublefome and chargeable to this kingdom.

This was defigned in part by Queen Elizabeth and King James, and perhaps had been effected for the whole, but that the Irifh could not be faid to have been fully conquered before the tenth year of his reign, which was after the making of thofe ftatutes. It would be, I confefs, an advantage to England to be freed from the charge and neceffity of keeping that kingdom under by a conftant army; and, confidering the inconveniences this nation has fuffered by their frequent wars and rebellions, their gain would be more if they had never conquered the country in which the loffes of the Englifh could perhaps be never better compenfated than by finking it, if poffible, under water. The acceffion of fo much people unto England might make fome reparation for the greater number which to our own impoverifhment we have fent thither. I have dwelt the longer upon the confiderations of Scotland and Ireland to fhow the Frenchman may be miftaken who, about ten or twelve years since, published a book of politics chalking out the way for the French king's gaining the universal monarchy, (in imitation of Campanella to Philip the Second on the same subject,) wherein, after several insufferable flights and indignities, intolerable, base, false and malicious characters thrown and fixed upon the English, he tells it will be an easy task to overcome them, (but in the last place,) by sowing divisions among the king of England's subjects, especially those of Scotland and Ireland, by false insinuations, jealousies and fears of Popery and arbitrary government, &c.; the prevention whereof will be his Majesty's particular care, and the Parliament's, to enable him to carry on this great work of our common safety against the common enemy, the disturber of the peace of Christendom, by finding out an easy and sufficient fund.

Chapter XIII.

OF TAXES.

THIS naturally brings me to the consideration of taxes, allowed by all understanding men as absolutely necessary for the support of the body politic, as meat and drink for the natural. But what kinds are best has been much disputed. Before I descend to particulars, it is not amiss to observe in general that no taxes can be just or safe which are not equal. All subjects, as well the meanest as the greatest, are alike concerned in the common safety, and therefore should, according to their respective interests of riches or enjoyments, bear the charge in equal proportions. The contrary practice must of necessity beget murmurings and discontents, which seldom ending in words, proceed higher to blows, dividing the oppressed against the others, which will certainly disquiet and disturb, and may probably ruin both.

All taxes should be proportioned to the necessities of state, so that in computing these, the error, if any must be, is safer on the right hand than in defect; because the overplus may be ordered to other good public uses.

Further, when taxes are made equal to the people, and proportionate to the charges of the public, it is much more for the subject's ease and the common safety that they be made perpetual than temporary; for, if the means of securing ourselves against all the dangers to which we are exposed be not sufficient, we must undoubtedly yield ourselves up to the mercy of our enemies, or suffer much vexation in parting with further supplies from time to time out of that substance which nature, or our own almost equally binding customs have made but just enough for the support of ourselves and

Of Taxes.

families, either of which is very grievous. Becaufe alfo the event is uncertain, it is hard to determine which of the two is moft deftructive to the pleafures of life; for he that fays the choice is eafy, in that your enemies may take away your life, the other courfe does but render it miferable, is in my opinion much miftaken, it being more eligible to have no fenfe at all than to have it only to endure pain; for life is in itfelf a thing indifferent, neither good nor bad but as it is the fubject of pleafing or unpleafing perceptions; and is then better or worfe as it has more or lefs of the one or the other: fo that the proper queftion is not, whether it be better to live or not to live? but, whether mifery be preferable to no mifery? to which not only reafon but fenfe is able to give a fatisfactory anfwer. You fee then, that if the taxes fall fhort of their end, we are expofed to great miferies; and therefore to exceed is fafer, efpecially when things may be fo ordered that after the occafions are fupplied, the furplufage may be refunded or employed in the way of a bank or lombard or public trade, as fishing or clothing, &c.

The first, as an unexpected gift, will be very grateful to the people, and the other will not be less beneficial because it must increase their riches, and be a fund, without new taxes, for any future emergencies.

That perpetuating the revenue is most easy for the people and most convenient for public ends, will farther appear from these following considerations; that an equal tax, though greater than is needful, so the money be not hoarded up to hinder trade, but issued as fast as it comes in, for necessaries within the country, however it may for the present make some alterations in particular families, does not impoverish the whole: for riches, as power, consisting in comparison, all equally retrenching some part of their expenses, remain as rich as they were before. This retrenchment may at first seem unpleasant and stomachful to those who think what they have little enough for their private expense; but such ought to consider, if they refuse to

Of Taxes.

part with some, they will infallibly lose all; that instead of being a free people, they may become slaves, and will not then have it in their power to keep ought of what they call their own; have no liberty or property, but at the pleasure of their conquering triumphant lord and master: that then they will be dealt with like beasts, now they have the liberty of rational men, *i.e.* of choosing with the wise merchant in a storm, to throw some of his goods overboard, to secure his life and the rest of his fortune. When by prudent rules of economy and temperance they have pared off those great extravagances men are now given to, in clothes, in meat and drink, &c., to the decay of their healths and shortening of their lives, and have proportioned their layings-out to their comings-in, what for the present seems so hard will become very easy, and be hereafter no more felt than the payment of tithes now; which without doubt wrought the same effect at first as this may be supposed to do. But what is yet much better, they will make us rich; for I am

Of Taxes.

convinced that the great taxes in the united Netherlands, have been the chiefeft caufe of their great wealth; and though this be no fmall paradox, and perhaps a new one, I am fully perfuaded it contains a great truth; for their great taxes neceffitated great induftry and frugality, and thefe becoming habitual, could not but produce wealth; efpecially confidering that the product of labour is more valuable to the kingdom than the land, and all other perfonal eftate, which I will fhow under the particular of trade. When the taxes are lefs than ferve, or to laft but for a time, thofe who do not make their expenfes fhort of their incomes, but think they may without prejudice make both ends meet; or if they exceed, fo foon as that proportion which now goes to the public comes in, it will make things even again; do not confider how difficult it is to fall, and that in the mean time an accident may happen that not only requires the continuance of the temporary, but alfo of impofing new and greater taxes: then, when perhaps it is too late, they cry out they are ruined and undone; and indeed, the case seems hard, yet cannot be avoided. Therefore, to answer our present needs, and prevent for the future such great evils, the taxes are to be made perpetual; so we, being under a necessity of adjusting our private affairs accordingly, a little time will make them habitual to us, and insensible to our posterity: for, that if they be not perpetual, but to determine at certain or uncertain periods of time, they do not only become uneasy to the subject, but inconvenient for the public security, which may suffer much at home and abroad in the interval before new supplies can be legally raised.

I do not doubt but you and your fellow-members have it in your thoughts that all the customs and half the excise cease upon the death of our sovereign, for whose long life every good subject is bound by interest no less than duty heartily to pray; but is it not to be remembered that the period of human life is uncertain, though that of our

Of Taxes.

evil which may thereupon enfue, be not. The occafions of our expenfe continuing, though the means of fupporting them fail; before a parliament can be convened, thofe others may be increafed, becaufe in the meantime the merchants will fill the kingdom with goods, and fell them at the fame rates they now do, reckoning that a lucky hit; and fo anticipate the markets for two, three or more years, with all manner of ftaple commodities, linen, filk, falt, &c., which they have near at hand; and with what perifhable commodities they can procure, for as long a term as they will laft, and perhaps covetoufly and foolifhly for a longer. Thus the people will pay and lofe, and yet the ftate grow poor, as well for the prefent, as future, while the merchants only, the overhafty and immature, will have the profit: and though they talk loudeft, the confumptioner ftill pays the duty, and that with intereft.

In proportioning of taxes, we muft have recourfe to the neceffities of the charge, which

Of Taxes.

in my sense of things ought to extend to all that relate to us as single persons in matters of right or wrong, as law, &c., as well as to what concerns us with references to the whole in our public occasions, as of peace or war, foreign or domestic. For I hold it altogether as reasonable that the public should pay all those officers who promote and distribute justice, as well as those others now paid by the state; in proportion to which I hope our governors will consider what will suffice for the management of all affairs that any way conduce to the joint good of the whole body politic, and when that is known and fixed, leave the rest to our own particular disposal.

But in this proportioning of taxes we must rather look forward than backward. Our home occasions are easily judged, but those abroad must be taken by other measures, the former use of money compared with its present, the ancient demesnes of the crown with what they are now, and the strength and power of our neighbours, especially the

Of Taxes.

French; concerning whom we are not to forget that that crown is much more potent than it was heretofore by the acceffion of large territories, which, when England's, gave it great aid and affiftance in their war. The expenfe of one year's war in this age is greater than that of twenty in former times, when twopence a day would go further than twenty pence now; when fix or ten thoufand men were as confiderable an army as forty or fifty thoufand now; when a fmall caftle, moat, or ordinary ditch, was a good fortification, but mighty baftions, large curtains doubly fortified with fausfbrais, counterfcarps, half-moons, redoubts, and great variety of other outworks, according to the nature and fituation of places, with exquifite fkill and vaft expenfe made and defended, together with the ftrongeft citadels, are now taken. Then the charges of arms and ammunition, bows and arrows ferving inftead of fire-arms, were inconfiderable; but now France has in conftant pay above 120,000, fome fay above 200,000, fighting men, whofe ftanding army

Of Taxes.

in former times exceeded not 10,000, nor so many but on particular occasions, when a single battle, or at most a summer's expedition put an end to a war, no long nor formal sieges to spin out the quarrel. Now the whole scene is changed from what in those days it consisted in; courage and strength of body into that where patience in fatigue, dexterity in wit, and money in purse shall make the coward and the weak an equal match, at least, for sinewy and gigantic force. There is no doubt, that as many of the English as luxury and idleness have not softened into effeminacy, have still as great valour and resolution; but they are to consider that their old enemies the French are not the same they formerly were; that they (finding their first *sa-sa* or brisk onset would not do the feat, and wanting courage to rally, nature having denied them bodily strength, but to supply that defect having given them wit to use stratagems,) have quite changed the scene of war, and taken their leave of the old way of venturing body to body.

Of Taxes.

In Queen Elizabeth's time thirty ships, such as perhaps exceeded not our third and fourth-rate frigates, were the fleet which gave law to the biggest part of the world, the sea; and without the help of storms doubted not to have overcome the too arrogantly styled Invincible Armada. In those days few besides the kingdom of Spain and state of Venice had any ships of war; France and Holland were then very weak, and all four unable to contend with us. Now the Swedes, Danes, Hamburghers, Ostenders, and Algerines, &c., have considerable fleets; the states of the United Provinces have much more shipping than the French king, who yet has upwards of two hundred men-of-war, and many larger than most in Europe, and is every day building more; and lest he should yet have further need, I have an account, he has lately countermanded about fifty sail of St. Malo's and Havre de Grace merchant-men, of considerable force, bound to Newfoundland. If then his power be so vastly increased that, as he gives out, he has cash for five years' charge, and provisions and forage for two; that his ordinary revenue in France, not to speak of his new acquisitions, amounts by the most modest computation to above nine millions sterling per annum; and his country being rich, and the power in his own hands, he may at any time raise what more he pleases. Is it not then necessary to consider our own strength, and by sufficient supplies at home as well as allies abroad secure our necks against that yoke with which he threatens to enslave all Europe?

Nor will it be amiss for the subject to observe that the French by fomenting our quarrels, foreign and domestic, have been the main occasions of the great taxes and impositions, (necessary appendages of the former,) under which the English nation has groaned for these last forty years. Even the ship-money had its rise from the affronts their pride and insolence threw upon us; and they will yet oblige us to suffer more, unless by the joint force of our arms and money in a round

Of Taxes.

and large supply for the war, we speedily enable ourselves to revenge our past injuries and their present designs, and so put it out of their power, either by this or any other of their crafty practices, to disturb or hurt us for the future.

And it is to be considered that as the expenses abroad are much greater, so they are likewise at home;—that an hundred pound before the eighteenth of Edward the Third was equivalent in intrinsic value to three hundred pound of our now current money; their groat being raised to our shilling. Also our expenses are not only far greater than they were in those days, but our necessary uses require ten times as much as they could be then supplied for; perhaps, no less occasioned by the discovery of the West Indian mines (the plenty of every commodity making it cheap), than by our own much greater extravagance: whence it is plain that the present revenue of the state, even for necessary occasions, ought to exceed the ancient, as thirty does one. And since our

160   *Of Taxes.*

great intereſt, no leſs than honour, lies in ſecuring the dominion of the ſeas, and by that our trade, our fleet muſt be anſwerable to that of our neighbours; it will then, allowing the Engliſh, man to man, to be a third ſtronger than the French, ſeem reaſonable to have an hundred and fifty ſhips of war in conſtant readineſs. And comparing the charge of the Admiralty, by taking an eſtimate of what it was in Queen Elizabeth's time, 30,000*l.*, and in the beginning of King James's, 1604, 40,000*l.*, with what it has been ſince this king's reign, which, if I miſtake not, I have been told by more than yourſelf, was offered to be made out in Parliament to have been 500,000*l.* per annum; but granting it was but 400,000*l.* it muſt follow that our fleet has been ten times bigger than that of King James, or that the charge is now ten times more. Hence if it be yet neceſſary to enlarge it treble to make it ſtrong enough, that will increaſe the ordinary annual charge by the firſt account to 1,500,000*l.*, by the laſt to 1,200,000*l.* And if the building of thirty ships require near 600,000*l.*, how much more will be wanting to complete the fleet, 150 sail, and to continue building every year, with an allowance of one third less in proportion to the French king's? by which we cannot yet reckon ourselves secure from the common foe without a strict alliance with the Germans, Dutch and Spaniards. If then the ordinary occasions of our fleet require thus much, and the extraordinary a vast addition, the common expenses in every particular being thirty for one, more than in Edward the Third's time, when the crown had a large revenue in lands, what will all need in the extraordinary accidents of war, &c. now when these are almost dwindled into nothing? But these considerations I leave to the proper persons; yet, by the bye, give me leave to tell you they were never thought of by those malcontents who have talked loudly of the great supplies this king has had. This alone cancels the obligation; he that brags of having done another good turns, pays himself, and does not only free, but disoblige the receiver. It would have argued more ingenuity not to have compared the fubfidies of this king's reign with thofe of his predeceffors, without taking notice that perhaps his occafions required more than all theirs did;—that during the eighteen years he and his father were kept out of their rights, he muft have contracted vaft debts for the fupport of himfelf, his army, and his followers;—that the great revenue of the crown was in a manner gone;—that other kings had fqueezed vaft fums from their fubjects by loans, monopolies, &c. of which no mention was made in the computation;—and that the building of fhips, and above four years of fuch a war at fea, confumed more than any one hundred years' war on land fince the Conqueft. The confideration of the vaft charge Dunkirk put the crown to—at leaft three times more than it yielded—occafioned the advice of its fale. Tangier too has ftood the king in very great fums; and till of late the fupporting the charge of Ireland helped to drain the exchequer of

England; whilft the intrinfic value of one million formerly was equal to that of three millions now, and in real ufe to thirty millions; for the true intrinfic value or worth of money is no otherwife to be computed than according to what it will purchafe for our prefent confumptions, which I have reckoned to exceed thofe of old only by ten, though I have heard others fay much more. But that which has made thefe complaints fo loud, has not been only inconfideration or, perhaps, malice, but the inequality of impofing the taxes; and thofe great inconveniences may be eafily obviated for the future by making and applying to particular ufes fuch fufficient and equal funds as are neceffary to be fettled. I will only inftance in one, that of the cuftoms, which feems originally to have had its rife for that end; and therefore ought to be appropriated to the ufe of the navy. I wifh it were great enough for fuch as our fafety requires.

And if this courfe be taken in apportioning the revenue, the public and private expenfes

Of Taxes.

are to be generously computed. The doing so will remove jealousies and distrusts on all sides, the king will be under no necessity of straining his prerogative, by hearkening to the devices of projectors; the people will be quiet and at ease; and then every man may safely sit under his own vine and his own fig-tree, and enjoy with pleasure the fruits of his labour. If you look into the histories of past ages, you will find the disputes of the prerogative on one hand, and of liberty on the other, were always founded on the want of money; and he that considers the evils that have ensued, will soon believe it very necessary to prevent the like for the future, by applying to every use of the crown or state (I do not say to the person of the king, whose greatest share is the trouble, while the subject's is security and ease) a sufficient and perpetual revenue. This act will beget an entire confidence and love, and so unite us to one another, as will make it impossible for any storms without, or commotions within, to shake this kingdom so founded on a rock;

Of Taxes.

against which all who make any attempts must needs split themselves and fortunes.

I have, according to my wonted freedom, given you my thoughts why I think it more convenient, both for public and private, that the revenue were sufficient and perpetual. Against this I never met but with one objection, to wit, that if that were done, the king would not so frequently, if at all, call his Parliament: as if there were no use for this great council but raising of money. The altering or repealing the old, and making new laws; the reforming of errors and abuses in inferior courts of justice; the deciding the controversies those courts could not, and many other things would make their meeting necessary. The king would see it were his advantage to call them often, since besides that there is safety in the multitude of counsellors, all that happens to be severe and harsh would light on them, and yet none could be offended because the act of the whole. Nor could his Majesty but be sensible that all innovations are dangerous in a

Of Taxes.

state; for it is like a watch, out of which any one piece lost would disorder the whole. The Parliament is the great spring or heart without which the body of the commonwealth could enjoy neither health nor vigour, life nor motion. While they mind their duty in proposing and advising what is best for king and people, without private respect, leaving him the undoubted prerogative of kings, of Nature and reason, of assenting or dissenting, as he is convinced in his conscience is best for the common good, which is to be his measure in all actions, as the laws are to be the subject's rule, I see not why it should not be his interest to call them frequently. None can be supposed to advise the contrary, unless some few great men, to avoid not so much perhaps the justice as the passion, envy and prejudice of some in that judicature to whom they may think themselves obnoxious; but granting this, it is unreasonable to think so wise and so good a prince will prefer the private interest of any single man, though never so great, before the

Of Taxes. 167

general good and fatisfaction of his people. I fhould rather think he will, in the words of his royal father, in a fpeech to his Parliament, give in this a full affurance, " I muft conclude that I feek my people's happinefs, for their flourifhing is my greateft glory, and their affection my greateft ftrength." His Majefty well knows with what tendernefs and love his fubjects are to be treated; that it is more fafe, more pleafing, and more eafy, to erect his throne over their hearts than their heads, to be obeyed for love rather than fear. The dominion founded on the latter often meets the fame fate with a houfe built upon the fands, while that eftablifhed on the former continues firm and immovable as a rock. He is not ignorant, that as the multitude of the wife is the welfare of the world, fo does the being and well-being of the Englifh nation confift in the frequent counfels, deliberations and acts of King and Parliament, in which Providence has fo blended the king and people's interefts, that like hufband and wife they can never be fundered without

Of Taxes.

mutual inconvenience and unhappinefs. The fenfe and obfervation of this makes our king's reign profperous, and gives him a more glorious title than that of king, viz. the father of the country, and the great God-like preferver of his children's rights and liberties, who, out of a deep fenfe of duty and gratitude, muft own and remember who tells them that a wife king is the upholding of his people; and therefore cannot but pay him, even for their own intereft, all imaginable loyalty, deference, and refpect, giving up their lives and fortunes for his (or, which is all one, their own) fafety, who ftudies nothing fo much as their good and welfare. Befides, the king has already paffed an Act that a Parliament fhall fit at leaft once in three years, and in feveral fpeeches he has declared himfelf ready to do what further we fhall defire for the better fecurity of our liberties, properties and religion; why then fhould any think he would not efteem it his own as well as people's intereft to confult often, and upon all fudden occafions, with his Parliament? For

Of Taxes.

my own part, I should rather believe, by continuing this so long, that he would not be against their assembling thrice a year, as by the grace of former kings was accustomed for many years, before and after the Conquest. But, to put all jealousies to silence, the Parliament, in settling and appropriating the revenue to particular uses, may (as they have already begun to do in the Act for building thirty ships) grant it under a kind of condition or proviso, viz. that the respective officers give a full account of the employment thereof unto the Parliament at least once in every three years; otherwise all farther levies of the same to cease, &c.

Having said thus much in general of taxes, I come now to the particular branches; I have already showed the inconvenience of the customs, &c. determining with the king's life; I will further add that the book of rates ought to be reviewed, and in the new one a greater consideration had of the usefulness and necessity of the commodities in placing the imposition on them; viz. rating all the

Of Taxes.

allowed commodities of France much higher than they are, raifing the duty of their wines, to be at leaft equal with that on thofe of Spain. I never yet could be fatisfied what induced the compilers of that book to rate Spanifh wines higher than thofe of France; fince the height of duty is a fort of prohibition which ought to be more taken care of in the trade with France, by which we are vaft lofers, than in that with Spain, which is a gainful one. The beft reafon I could find is that they did it inconfiderately, taking it as they found it left by the Long Parliament, who, by the fenfe of revenge for the war, were induced fo to treat the Spaniard. One might have thought the laft impoft on French wines would have leffened their importation, which Colbert, the financier, obferving it had not done (I was affured at my return in Auguft, by Fontainbleau, that) in his meafures for the next year's charge, he valued his mafter 100,000*l.* on that account, not doubting but the Parliament would take off that duty of wine which would give him

Of Taxes.

opportunity to put fo much on; that at this the French king fmiled and faid, " for fuch a kindnefs he fhould be obliged, and would no more call them *petite maifon*." But I hope, notwithftanding his fcornful quibble, he will find fuch fober refolutions in that houfe, as will fet him a madding, and that inftead of taking off that duty he may perceive more put on; which is indeed the only effectual way to prohibit the importation of thofe vaft quantities of French goods by which England is greatly impoverifhed. To leffen the traffic of his people is the firft ftep to lower him; which I am perfuaded is beft done by impofing an exceffive high duty upon all the commodities, and contriving the Act fo that nothing fhould pafs duty free. This courfe would be a better reftraint than abfolute prohibition. And it is the method he himfelf has taken in the trade with us, which he had long fince wholly forbid, but that upon examination he found it was driven to above 1,600,000*l*. advantage to his fubjects and lofs to thofe of England. This,

Of Taxes.

rather yearly increasing than decreasing, will at length quite ruin us if not prevented; and yet notwithstanding he imposes upon our cloths four shillings an ell, as a sumptuary law to oblige his subjects to the use of their own manufactures.

The next is the Excise, which, if equally imposed, were the best and easiest of all taxes; and to make it so, after the manner of Holland, it ought to be laid upon all things ready to be consumed. This puts it into the power of every man to pay more or less, as he resolves to live loosely or thriftily; by this course no man pays but according to his enjoyment or actual riches, of which none can be said to have more than what he spends; true riches consisting only in the use. But the present excise is grievous because heavier on the poor labourers and meaner sort of people than on the rich and great, who do not pay above a tenth of what the others do; and considering that most of the noble and private families out of London brew their own drink, it falls yet heavier on the poorer

Of Taxes.

fort, and will at laſt on the State; for the common brewers do already complain that they daily loſe their trade, many of their cuſtomers, even in London, brewing for themſelves to ſave the impoſition. To ſpeak the truth in good conſcience, this branch ought to have been impoſed on the nobles and eſtated-men rather than on the artificer and labourers, who were very ſlenderly concerned in the grounds of it, viz. the taking away the wardſhips and purveyance, which was ſo great an advantage to the public, eſpecially the richer, that that act of grace and condeſcenſion in his Majeſty, which freed us and our poſterity from great inconveniences and greater ſigns of ſubjection ought never to be forgotten.

This Act gave us a greater propriety and liberty than ever we had before; and muſt the poor chiefly pay for the benefit of the rich? let it not be told to the generations to come that an Act ſo unequal was contrived by thoſe who ſtudy only the public intereſt. I pray then let it be reviewed, and either made general on all public and private brewers, (by which the rich will ftill have advantage of the poor, according to the difference between ftrong and fmall beer; for to allow public brewers, and prohibit all private ones, as is practifed in the Low Countries, would never be endured in England) or rather let it be placed on malt, or taken quite off, and laid on the land as a perpetual crown rent; or let there be a general excife, the moft equal tax that poffibly can be devifed, on all confumed commodities of our own growth, or imported; which ought to be managed by proper officers, the farming of any part of the revenue being of evil confequence, as I could fhow at large, both to the State and people.

The hearth-money is a fort of excife, but a very unequal one too; the fmoke on it has offended the eyes of many, and it were to be wifhed that it were quite taken away and fomething in lieu thereof given to the crown lefs offenfive to the people's fenfes. I have heard many fay that an impofition on li-

Of Taxes.

cenfes for felling of ale, ftrong waters, coffee, cider, mum, and all other liquors, and for victualling-houfes, might be as beneficial to the crown, and fo ordered as might prevent or difcover highwaymen, &c. I have read among the Irifh ftatutes one to this purpofe, obliging among other things the inn-keepers, &c., to make good all horfes ftolen out of their ftables or paftures. An impofition on all ftage-coaches, carts, wagons, and carriers, fet afide for the well ordering the roads, would be of general advantage, as would a tax upon periwigs, ferving in part as a fumptuary law. A year, or half a year's rent charged upon all the new buildings fince 1656 would not only much oblige the City of London, enabling them by the difference of rents to let thofe many wafte houfes, which now, to the ruin of trade, remain untenanted, but alfo gratify the kingdom by eafing them from the common, threadbare land tax.

I do not queftion but, in this conjuncture, the wit of men will be contriving new ways

Of Taxes.

to supply the present occasions of a war; for that a land tax is slow and unequal; and I am apt to fancy that of the poll-money will be pitched upon as the most speedy levy, but must not be too great. As to myself, I am not solicitous what course they take, but wish it such as may be equal, and so will be pleasing to most; but be it great or small, the king as formerly will be again defrauded unless there be special care taken. The way I apprehend is, that for twenty-one years to come, neither plaintiff nor defendant be allowed the benefit of the law, without producing an authentic acquittance or discharge that they have paid this poll-money, and averring the same in their actions or pleas;— that the ministers be forbid to marry within that space any who do not, women as well as men, produce such certificates;—that none be admitted to any office or command, civil or military, administration or executorship, freedom or privilege in town, city, or corporation, or received into any of the public schools, inns, or universities, if of the age

Of Taxes.

limited by the act, except they make out the said payment; which in three months after ought to be regiftered, with the perfons' names and qualities.

Now, in regard that England is already very much under peopled, and will be more fo if there be a war; to provide againft thofe evils, and to obviate in fome meafure the loofenefs and debauchery of the prefent age, I have thought of a fort of tax which I believe is perfectly new to all the world, and under which it is probable, if it takes, I have made provifion for my own paying the crown no inconfiderable fum during my life.

It is a tax upon celibate, or upon unmarried people, *viz.* that the eldeft fons of gentlemen, and other degrees of nobility upwards, fhould marry by twenty-two complete, all their daughters by eighteen, and younger fons by twenty-five: all citizens' eldeft fons (not gentlemen) by twenty-three, all other men by twenty-five: all the daughters (not fervants) of all men under the degree of gentlemen, to marry by nineteen; all maid-servants by twenty—that all widowers under fifty marry within twelve months after the death of their wives; all widows under thirty-five, within two years after their husbands' decease, unless the widowers or widows have children alive. I allow the women, as the softer and better natured, more time to lament their loss—that no man marry after seventy nor widow after forty-five—that all men co-habit with their wives.

The eldest sons of gentlemen, and all other degrees of nobility upwards, and all other persons not married by the times limited as aforesaid, shall pay per annum a-piece these following rates, *viz*:—

Dukes, marquesses, and their eldest sons forty pound, other lords and their eldest sons twenty pound, knights, baronets ten pound, esquires eight pound, gentlemen five pound, citizens three pound, all other retailing tradesmen two pound—the younger brothers or sons of all the foregoing persons respectively half so much; and likewise the maiden

Of Taxes.

daughters, or rather their fathers or guardians for them—servants, labourers, and others six shillings and eight pence.

All the above-said widowers or widows, not marrying again under the age aforesaid, shall pay half; but marrying again after the ages above limited, double according to their qualities respectively; and all married men not cohabiting with their wives to pay quadruple.

You may perceive I do not forget, in this scheme, to practise some of the courtesy of England towards the women; that in regard it is not fashionable for them to court (an hardship, custom and their own pride have foolishly brought upon them), they are taxed but at half what their elder brothers are.

These things I do not set down with a design of giving people a liberty of playing the fool, as now, by irregular lives under those penalties. For all single persons that do so, I would have obliged under an indispensable necessity to marry one another; and I could wish a further severity of punishment were inflicted upon adultery by the state, since it is so much neglected by the church.

It would also be of great and public advantage that all marriages were celebrated openly in the church, according to the canon or rubric, and the banns three several sundays or holydays first published; but if this must be still dispensed with, that then all dukes and marquesses, and their eldest sons should pay twenty pound, all noblemen and their eldest sons fifteen pound, every knight and his eldest son seven pound ten shillings, every gentleman or others five pound, to the king as a public tax for such licenfe over and above the present established fee in the consistory court. If all children may not be baptized openly in the church, the births of all, even Non-conformists, should be duly registered. The knowing the exact numbers of the people would be of great advantage to the public weal, and conduce to many good and noble purposes, which (for brevity' sake) I omit to mention.

Chapter XIV.

OF TRADE.

THIS courſe may perhaps prevent many inconveniences that young men and women bring upon themſelves and the public; and ſince the *Concubitus Vagus* is acknowledged to hinder procreation, the reſtraint thereof will be one means of advancing TRADE, by adding more people to the common-wealth, which, perhaps, in the following particulars you will find to be the greateſt occaſion of its decay, an inconvenience by all poſſible means to be removed; for that trade is the ſupport of any kingdom, eſpecially an iſland, enabling the ſubjects to bear the taxes, and ſhewing them ways of living more agreeable than thoſe of the ſavage Indians in America, whoſe con-

Of Trade.

dition is but a few degrees diftant from that of brutes. Since then it is fo neceffary, it deferves the Parliament's beft care to reftore it to what it has been, or make it what it fhould be. The firft thing to be done is, the erecting a Council or Committee of Trade, whofe work fhould be to obferve all manner of things relating thereunto, to receive informations of all tradefmen, artificers and others, and thereupon make their obfervations; to confider all the ftatutes already made, and out of them form fuch bill or bills as fhall be more convenient, and prefent them to the Parliament to be enacted.

There are already many difcourfes publifhed; fome of them would be worth their view, and, did they fit conftantly, many would bring their remarks; and I myfelf fhould be able to give fome notions on this fubject, which, for want of time, I cannot now give you.

The two great principles of riches are land and labour; as the latter increafes, the other grows dear; which is no otherwife done

Of Trade.

than by a greater confluence of induſtrious people; for where many are coop'd into a narrow ſpot of ground, they are under a neceſſity of labouring, becauſe in ſuch circumſtances they cannot live upon the products of nature, and having ſo many eyes upon them, they are not ſuffered to ſteal; whatever they ſave of the effects of their labour, over and above their conſumption, is called riches; and the bartering or commuting thoſe products with others is called trade; whence it follows that not only the greatneſs of trade or riches depends upon the numbers of people, but alſo the dearneſs or cheapneſs of land, upon their labour and thrift.

Now, if trade be driven ſo that the imports exceed in value the exports, the people muſt of neceſſity grow poor, *i. e.* conſume the fundamental ſtock, *viz.* land and labour, both falling in their price. The contrary courſe makes a kingdom rich. The conſequence is that, to better the trade of England, the people (which will force labour) muſt be encreaſed, and thrift encouraged; for

Of Trade.

to hope for a vaft trade where people are wanting is not only to expect brick can be made without ftraw, but without hands.

The great advantage a country gains by being fully peopled you may find by the following obfervation, *viz.* That the value of the labour is more than the rent of the land, and the profit of all the perfonal eftates of the kingdom, which thus appears:—fuppofe the people of England to be fix millions, their annual expenfe at twenty nobles or fix pound thirteen and fourpence a head, at a medium for rich and poor, young and old, will amount to forty millions; and, if well confidered, cannot be eftimated much lefs. The land of England and Wales contains about twenty-four millions of acres, worth, one with another, about fix and eight pence per acre, or the third part of a pound; confequently the rent of the land is eight millions per annum. The yearly profit of all the people's perfonal eftate is not computed above eight millions more; both together make fixteen millions per annum: this taken out of the forty millions' yearly expenfe, there will remain twenty-four millions, to be fupplied by the labour of the people; whence follows that each perfon, man, woman and child, muft earn four pound a year, and an adult labouring perfon double that fum; becaufe a third part or two millions are children, and earn nothing; and a fixth part or one million by reafon of their eftates, qualities, callings or idlenefs, earn little; fo that not above half the people working muft gain, one with another, eight pounds per annum a-piece, and, at twenty years' purchafe, will be worth eighty pounds per head. For, though an *individuum* of mankind be reckoned but about eight years' purchafe, the fpecies is as valuable as land; being in its own nature perhaps as durable and as improveable too, if not more fo, increafing ftill fafter by generation, than decaying by death; it being very evident that there are much more yearly born than die. Whence you may plainly perceive, how much it is the intereft of the ftate, and therefore ought to be their care and study, to fill the country with people: the profit would not be greater in point of riches, than in strength and power; for it is too obvious to be insisted on, that a city of one mile in circumference and ten thousand men, is twice as strong and easier defended than one of four miles with double the number.

Now there are but two ordinary ways of increasing the people, that of generation and that of drawing them from other countries: the first is a work of time, and though it will not presently do our business, yet is not to be neglected. I have shown how it may be hastened by obliging to marriage, and more might be added by erecting hospitals for foundlings after the manner now used in other countries, and practised with great advantage in Paris, by the name of *L'Hostel pour les Enfants Trouvés*, where there are now reckoned no less than four thousand. This in all parts of England, especially London, would prevent the many murders and contrived abortions now used, not only to the

Of Trade.

prejudice of their fouls' health but that of their bodies alfo, and to the general damage of the public. This would likewife be an encouragement to the poorer fort to marry, who now abftain, to prevent the charge of children.

Strangers are no otherwife to be invited than by allowing greater advantages than they have at home; and this they may with more eafe receive in England than in any part of Europe, where natural riches do much abound, *viz.* corn, flefh, fifh, wool, mines, &c. and which Nature has bleffed with a temperature of healthful air, exceeding all northern, and not inferior to moft fouthern countries—has given it commodious ports, fair rivers, and fafe channels, with poffibilities of more for water carriage: thefe, with what follows, would foon make England the richeft and moft powerful country of the world. Naturalization without charge, plain laws and fpeedy juftice, freedom in all corporations, immunities from taxes and tolls for feven years, and laftly, liberty of confcience; the reſtraint of which has been the greateſt cauſe at firſt of unpeopling England, and of its not being ſince repeopled. This drove ſhoals away in Queen Mary's, King James, and King Charles the Firſt's days. It has loſt the wealth of England many millions, and been the occaſion of ſpilling the blood of many, many thouſands of its people. It is a ſad conſideration that Chriſtians ſhould be thus fooled by obſtinate religioniſts, in whom too much ſtiffneſs on one ſide and folly and perverſeneſs on the other, ſhould have been equally condemned. Both are indeed the effects of pride, paſſion or private intereſt, and altogether foreign to the buſineſs of religion; which, as I have already told you, conſiſts not in a belief of diſputable things (of which if either part be true, neither are to us neceſſary), but in the plain practice of piety, which is not incompatible with errors in judgment. I ſee not, therefore, why the clergy ſhould be wholly hearkened to in this affair, ſince it is really impertinent to the truth of religion; and I dare appeal to all the ſober underſtanding and confiderative men of the Church of England, whether the oppofition of this be not wholly founded upon intereft, which being but of particular men ought not, nor will not, I hope, weigh more with the Parliament than that of the public, which is fo highly concerned in this matter.

And though it may be objected that as affairs of religion now ftand, none need leave England for want of toleration, yet certain I am, without it none will return or come in anew. And if our neighbours thrive and increafe in people, trade and wealth, we continuing at a ftay or growing ftill poorer and poorer, by that means rendered unable to refift a foreign power, are like to fall into fuch hands as will force us to worfhip God after the way which almoft all of us now call herefy, and many idolatry. Which induces me to conclude that nothing but inconfideration can move even the clergy to oppofe this thing, on which their own as well as the fafety of all others does fo very much depend.

But in regard the defects of trade cannot

Of Trade.

prefently be fupplied by bringing in more people, becaufe a work of time, it is neceffary to make thofe we have ufeful, by obliging the idle and unwilling to a neceffity of working, and by giving the poor that want it a full employment. This will in effect be a great increafing of the people, and may be eafily compaffed if workhoufes be erected in feveral parts of the kingdom, and all perfons forced into them who cannot give a fatisfactory account of their way of living. This would prevent robbing, burglary, and the cheats of gaming, counterfeiting of hands, money-clipping, &c. by which our lives and fortunes would be much better fecured. This would put men's wits upon the rack; hunger which eats through ftone walls, would make them in getting their livings by the fweat of their brows, mafters of art,* a degree perhaps more ufeful to the commonwealth than thofe of the univerfity. This would put them upon the invention of engines, whereby their labour would not only become more eafy but

* "Magifter artis ingenique largitor, venter."

Of Trade.

more productive of real advantages to the whole; rendering the poet's fable of Briareus's hundred hands a certain truth; one man doing more by an inftrument than fifty or a hundred without it. Wit will thus in fome meafure make amends for the want of people; yet fo dull and ignorant, fo infenfible of their own good are the vulgar, that generally inftead of being pleafed they are at firft almoft implacably offended at fuch profitable inventions. But it appears the Parliament had another fenfe of things, in that they allowed the advantage of fourteen years to the inventor: which law, with fubmiffion, might be altered to better purpofe if, inftead of a fourteen years' monopoly, fome reward out of the public ftock were given to the ingenious. The many fupernumeraries in divinity, law and phyfic, with which the kingdom (efpecially London) fwarms; all mountebanks, and pretenders to aftrology, together with the fupernumeraries in all manner of retailing trades (even the trade of merchandizing has too many hands) efpecially

Of Trade.

all pedlers or wanderers that carry their shops on their backs, lap-women, &c. who contribute little or nothing to the charge of the State, should be pared off and made useful to the public; to which, by the vast increase of these, the great number of idlers and beggars, not above two thirds even of the ordinary sort, can be looked upon as bringing in any real advantage; the other third, but like drones, living on the labour of the rest.

And to speak more freely, it is unreasonable and impolitic, especially in a great and over-grown city, to suffer any retail trades to be managed by men, when women, with the help of a few porters about the most cumbersome things, may do it much better. They will invite customers more powerfully than men can, and having nothing to do in the way of their shop trades, will not be idle, their needles employing them; while the men, perhaps from two, three, or four, to seven lusty young fellows, sit idle most part of their time, with their hands in their pockets, or blowing their fingers. Few of this sort of trades finding one with another, above two hours' work in the whole day; the men would study some more beneficial employments, and the women, having by this means something to do, would not as now, induced by idleness more than want, be occasions of so much wickedness and debaucheries, to the general prejudice of the Commonwealth, and the particular ruin of many good families.

To set on foot the fishing trade, allow all such as will undertake it, strangers or natives, the same benefits and privileges I have mentioned for the bringing in of the former; and I think if beyond that, houses were built for them in Lynn, or Yarmouth, &c., at the public charge, rent-free for seven years, every man would say it were for the general good who considers that this trade is the only basis of the grandeur and power that the States of Holland are no less lords of in Europe than in the East Indies, to which it has raised them in less than an hundred years, from the poor and distressed states to be one of the richest and mightieſt of the known world. This I could at large make appear, but that it having been done already, with the want of time, hinders me. I will only ſay that Holland has not the tenth part of thoſe natural conveniences for effecting this that England, Scotland, or Ireland has. Let the ſame encouragements be given to all ſuch, whether natives or foreigners, that ſhall jointly carry on the particular manufactures of iron, tin, earthenware, linen, &c. In the laſt, at three ſhillings and four pence an ell, one with another, there is reckoned conſumed by us above ſix hundred thouſand pounds; all which might be ſaved and the poor ſet at work by promoting that trade within ourſelves. To reſtore the woollen manufactures, almoſt decayed, take the ſame care in that and all other as the Dutch have done in that of the herrings; the neglect in this has been a main reaſon that our clothing trade is much leſſened. Reputation in commodities is as neceſſary as in the vendors, which makes the Dutch even at this day put on Engliſh marks, and thereby, for the ancient

Of Trade.

credit (now in a manner loft) ours were in, they have gained for their own manufactures the markets we want. The decay of our clothing traffic has been occafioned by feveral accidents; one, and no fmall one, is that of companies, which indeed are as much monopolies as if in one fingle perfon; they ruin induftry and trade, and, only to enrich themfelves, have a liberty by which they impoverifh the reft of the Commonwealth. Whatever reafon there was for firft erecting them, viz., to begin or carry on fome great undertaking which exceeded the power of particular men, there appears lefs or none now for their continuance. The enjoyment of liberty and property requires that all fubjects have equal benefit in fafety and commerce, and if all fubjects pay taxes equally, I fee no reafon why they fhould not have equal privileges.

And if part of thofe taxes be impofed for guarding the feas, I do really believe it would be more advantage to the king to fend convoys to the Eaft Indies, and to Guinea

Of Trade.

with any of his subjects trading thither, than to allow these two companies the sole benefit of engrossing those trades, though I think no others but they, being at considerable charge and expense, ought to be continued.

And since the East India and African Companies, especially the first, impose what rates they please upon their commodities, why should not they pay, for that power of taxing the subject, a considerable present proportion for carrying on the war, and a yearly round sum to the state, to ease the rest of the people who are debarred those advantages? In my opinion, gratitude to the king, as well as justice to the subject, should invite them to give a considerable standing yearly revenue to the crown. This may be policy too; for then perhaps they need never fear their dissolution, notwithstanding the clamours and many mouths now open against them.

But if it shall not be thought fit to take away all companies, why should it not be lawful once a year for any one that pleased

Of Trade.

to be made a member, paying in his quota? This, I confefs, would make it ufeful to the public, becaufe the trade would be managed by fewer hands, confequently to more profit, and every one being concerned, there could be no complaint.

But whatever is done in point of trade, particular corporations of artificers ought to be broken. They, as now managed, are encouragements to idlenefs, impofitions upon the reft of the people, and an unreafonable enflaving of apprentices, who in three years, for the moft part, may be as well mafters of their trade as in feven; but the advantage is, that when they come to fet up for themfelves, they commonly turn gentlemen, and cannot afford to fell a cabinet under fifteen pounds, becaufe they muft eat well and drink wine; though they own a Dutchman or a Frenchman that does not fo, may afford as good a one for twelve pounds. This of the cabinet is a late and a true ftory, and to my own experience. It is the fame in moft if not all other trades.

Of Trade.

The Fifhmongers' Company is of all others the greateft nuifance to the public, to the moft ufeful part thereof, the poor artificers and labourers; I was credibly informed at my laft being in London, by two fubftantial citizens, that they throw part of their fifh away, to inhance the value and price of the remainder.

For thefe and many more reafons I could give, it were convenient that every city and town corporate confifted but of one company, into which, without charge or formalities of freedom, every man, native or alien, ought to be admitted that pays his proportion of taxes and affeffments.

And in order to the bringing in foreigners, our native unmanufactured commodities ought to be ftrictly prohibited to other countries; more particularly the exportation of wool from England and Ireland ought to be reftrained; which will be better done by impofing a vaft duty upon it, as of thirty or forty fhillings a ftone or tod, than by making it felony: adding over and above great pe-

Of Trade.

cuniary mulcts, if shipped without payment of duty. If this were enacted, many would turn informers, who now out of tenderness of men's lives forbear the discovering this injurious practice: for prevention whereof great care ought to be taken, since the vast quantities of wool exported from England and Ireland into France and Holland have in a manner destroyed the great staple of England, the woollen manufacture, lowered the rents of land, and beggared thousands of people. By this the Dutch and French are enabled to make useful both their own and Spanish wools, which would otherwise be insignificant and ineffective of any considerable purposes; one being too fine, the other too coarse, without mixtures of English or Irish wool.

Those, by greater labour and frugality, who heretofore were furnished by us, do now not only supply themselves, but also undersell us abroad; and as if that injury were too little, we are content, by wearing their stuffs, to give them an opportunity of undermining

Of Trade.

us at home. If you confider thefe things ferioufly, you will with me be perfuaded it is not the great increafe of wool in England and Ireland that makes it a drug, but the practice of carrying it abroad, and our not being fatisfied to ape and mimic the French modes, but further to wear their ftuffs, though far inferior to our own.

I have heard it demonftrated by knowing men, that it would be England's great intereft to work up all their own and Irifh wool, though they fhould afterwards burn it when in ftuffs and cloth ; and I am convinced their doing fo one year would not only maintain the poor and habituate them to labour, but be as great an advantage in the fale of that manufacture both at home and abroad for the future, as the burning part of their fpices is to the Dutch. But I am of opinion there would be no need to burn any, for that which is now ufeful in wool would not be lefs fo in cloth. I have feen a computation by which it appears the working up all our own and Irifh wool, which England can do

Of Trade.

to better purpofes than a part, while the remainder is tranfported to other countries, would be many millions in the wealth of the people, and as many hundred thoufand pounds fterling in the king's coffers. For if we kept this commodity at home, we fhould not only give a full employment to our people, but neceffitate thofe who now in France and Holland maintain themfelves by this manufacture, fo foon as their ftocks were fpent, to find new arts of living, or elfe convey themfelves hither, which of the two is certainly the moft probable. Thus we fhould doubly increafe our wealth and our people; the latter by confequence raifing the rents and value of lands, in duplicate proportion (as I could demonftrate) to what they now yield. For a fhort inftance, obferve, that if there be a thoufand people in a country, the land whereof is worth a thoufand pounds per annum, and at twenty years' purchafe twenty thoufand pounds; if they be increafed half as many more, or to one thoufand five hundred people, the rent of the land will likewife be half as much more, *viz.* one thoufand five hundred pounds, and the number of years' purchafe not only twenty, but half as many more, *viz.* in all thirty; which makes the value of the inheritance amount to thirty times one thoufand five hundred, or forty-five thoufand pounds. The reafon of which is founded on this undeniable maxim, that land is more or lefs valuable as it is more or lefs peopled. When heretofore all the wool of England was manufactured in Flanders, it yielded but fixpence a pound; but foon after the reftraint of it in Edward the Third's time, the manufacturing all at home raifed it to eighteen-pence a pound, and brought into the kingdom great numbers of Flemings and Walloons. To encourage this further, all perfons whatfoever fhould wear nothing but ftuff and cloth of our own make, the ladies to have liberty to wear filk but in fummer. I am told that within thefe fix months, to encourage a woollen manufacture newly fet up in Portugal, no man, native or ftranger, is fuffered to appear at court in any other.

Of Trade.

That useful neglected act of burying in woollen should be strictly put in execution; not prohibiting the people, if they will be so foolish; but probably a little time will make them wiser than to throw away linen too, which if they would make at home might be the more tolerable. The way I conceive by which it may be easily done is to enjoin the minister under penalty of deprivation, with allowance of money to the informers, not to bury any one whose corpse or coffin they do not see covered with flannel. And since Death is said to be the sister of sleep, or rather since sleep is the representative of death as our beds are of our graves, or indeed that death is but a very long night, if we should not only bury but lie in flannel sheets, at least the long cold winter nights, I have been assured by our old friend that this practice, after a little use, would be found no less for the health, if not some voluptuousness of our natural bodies, than the other would prove for the body politic; and I am the more induced to believe this assertion, because physicians prescribe flannel shirts to some persons for their health. I am certain the more ways are found for the confumption of this manufacture, the richer our country would grow, by leffening the ufe of foreign linen, fo greatly advantageous to our neighbours of France; whom we love fo dearly that we ftudy how to ferve and enrich them, though to our own impoverifhment and ruin.

Befides this courfe, not a lock of wool fhould be permitted into the iflands of Jerfey, Guernfey, Alderney, or Sark; under colour of what is allowed, they are enabled to fupply their own occafions, and carry much more (of which I am well affured) to France, which reaps the benefit of the great induftry of thofe populous iflands. To make them beneficial, at leaft not hurtful, to England, is to deny them wool; if that would bring the people thence into this country, it would prove a double advantage. And laftly, I think the only certainty of keeping our wool from foreigners is to erect a company by the name of State Merchants, or oblige the Eaft India Company, whofe ftock and credit will enable them with eafe to buy up at good rates yearly all the wool of England and Ireland; which, manufactured at home, would bring them in a little time as profitable returns as thofe from Bantam, &c., be many millions in the riches of the people, by raifing the rents, &c., and hundreds of thoufands in the king's exchequer, employ thoufands of our poor now ftarving, and invite in many of other nations, to the great increafe of our ftrength and wealth, and fo prove no lefs a particular than an univerfal good.

All foreftallers, regraters, and higglers ought to be prevented, who now do as much mifchief to the City of London as formerly purveyance did the kingdom.

The prefent confufed bufinefs of weights and meafures, which appears by many ftatutes to have been the care of our anceftors, ought to be fully afcertained and adjufted. And becaufe this does greatly tend to the regulation of trade and adminiftration of juftice, it were convenient particular perfons were empowered who fhould receive complaints and correct abuses in those and all other penal statutes referring to trade by some more speedy course than that of information or indictment, &c.

No particular person or incorporations ought to have any places privileged against the king's writs.

The Parliament should be pleased to redress the great obstruction of justice by protections, of which no less than sixteen thousand are said to be given in and about London. I am persuaded that either the report is a mistake, or that the members' hands are counterfeited, for it is very unreasonable to believe the makers of our laws would prevent their execution; but be the case one way or other, the evil may be easily remedied by the members registering the names of their servants in the house at the beginning of the session and upon the alteration of any.

All manner of courts in corporations, whether by grant or prescription, ought to be taken away because of the many abuses daily committed; and in every corporation a court of merchants should be erected for the quick despatch and determination of all controversies relating to trade and commerce; every man should be obliged to tell his own story without charge or the assistance of attorneys or lawyers. The judges should be annually chosen, five in number, together with two registers, one for the Plaintiff, the other for the Defendant, out of the most experienced and best reputed citizens or tradesmen; no salary or fee to be paid to judge or officer.

Retrench by sumptuary laws the excessive wearing foreign silks, embroideries, and laces, and prohibit absolutely the use of silver and gold lace, gilding or lackering coaches, &c. When riches are thus not so much used as abused, it is no wonder they do not only moulder into dust but take wing (in Solomon's phrase) and fly away. Our wiser neighbours in France and Holland prevent this evil; the first make a show, but at an easy and cheap rate, the latter leave off their clothes because they are worn out, not that they are out of fashion. Our contrary practice in imported commodities makes us complain that trade is decaying, in which our folly has made us a byword among the French, as a people that confume our all on the back and the belly; and if none fpent more, the mifchief were but particular, but many are not contented to run out their own eftates, but refolve to have the pleafure of undoing others for company. So long as we indulge ourfelves in this vanity, we may indeed have the fatisfaction (if it be any) to talk of mending trade; but in fpite of our chat it will ftill decay, we fhall buy and fell more and more, and yet live by the lofs, till at laft we are wholly broken. How long that will be a doing we may guefs by the fall of the rents and value of lands, not to be avoided while the balance of trade is fo much greater on the imported fide than the exported. The way to make us rich is to manage our trade in the fame manner it was done in Edward the Third's time; to make the proportion of our exports exceed our imports as much as they then did. By an account taken in the feven and twentieth year of that king (as Cotton

Of Trade.

says) our exported commodities amounted to £294,184, the imported but £38,970; so that the kingdom got clear in that year £255,214, by which it appears that our present trade is about thirty times greater than it was then, though we complain of its fall; it is our own fault, we are so imprudent as to consume more of foreign goods than we sell of our own; this, I am convinced, we do in our French trade, it is well if we do not likewise play the fool in others. By the way, you may observe that if we would but moderate our expenses, we might very well bear our taxes, though they were near thirty times greater than in that king's reign, even with allowance for the alteration of coin.

The exportation of money in specie is so far from being a loss to the kingdom that it may be gainful, as it is to Leghorn and other places; and though we did not export any coin, yet we should not be the richer, since the over-balance would still lie as a debt upon our trade, which it must some time or other pay in that or another commodity, or otherwife break.

And the council or committee of trade may find out the wealth of the kingdom, which would ferve to many good purpofes, by making a yearly account of the goods imported and exported (beft known by the Cuftoms, as has been calculated by a friend of mine in another country). Thefe ought at leaft every feven years to be reviewed (fuppofing the life of commodities not longer than that of man); and, according to their alterations of ufefulnefs or neceffity to ourfelves or others the impofitions may be changed.

And here I muft take leave to affert that all imported commodities are better reftrained by the height of impofition than by an abfolute prohibition, if fufficient care be taken to oblige the importers to a full and ftrict payment; for this would be a kind of fumptuary law, putting a neceffity upon the confumer, by labour to enlarge his purfe, or by thrift to leffen his expenfe. And I am the more induced to this, by my obfervation that not-

Of Trade.

withstanding the several acts prohibiting the importation of many foreign commodities, yet nothing is more worn or used, especially the French, in which trade, if the overbalance (which is said to be above £1,600,000) were loaded with the charge of eight shillings in the pound, it would make the consumption of those commodities £640,000 dearer. If that would not restrain our folly, it would help to ease us in the public taxes; whereas now they are all imported without any other charge than what is paid for smuggling to tie up the seamen's tongues, and shut officers' eyes. To prevent this, it were fit that men were undeceived of the notion they have taken up, that the law does allow them their choice, either to pay the duty or the penalty if taken, which sure cannot be the end of any law which designs obedience and active compliance with what it enjoins, not a disobedience or breaking what it positively commands. If penal statutes be only conditional, then the traitor, the murderer or the thief, when he suffers the punifhment of difobedience, may be called an honeft man, and in another fignification than that of the Scotch phrafe, a juftified perfon. But the idle and unwarrantable diftinction of active and paffive obedience has done England greater mifchiefs. The revenue acts give not the fame liberty that thofe acts do which oblige the people to go to church, or to watch and ward under pecuniary mulcts. In thefe a power of choofing was defignedly left, which by many circumftances appears otherwife intended by the other. And, indeed, the practice is not only unjuft, but abufive to the whole body of the people, who pay as dear for what they buy as if the duty had been paid to the king, not put up in a few private men's pockets. It may likewife hinder trade, for if the fmuggler pleafe, he may underfell his neighbour who honeftly thinks it is a cheat and a fin not to give Cæfar his due; therefore a feal or fome private mark fhould be contrived for all forts of commodities, and power given to feize them when and wherever met, in merchants',

Of Trade.

retailers', or confumptioners' hands. And to prevent the paffing foreign commodities, as if made at home, for which, left any of thefe laft fhould pafs, they fhould in the town where they are made or expofed to fale, be firft marked or fealed in an office purpofely erected, without any delay or charge to the people.

That part of the act of navigation fhould be repealed which appoints three-fourths of the mariners to be Englifh: why not Scots, Irifh, or any of the king's fubjects, or even foreigners, fo the fhips do really belong to owners refident in England? We want people, therefore we ought to invite more, not reftrain any. This act is a copy of that made by the Long Parliament and their general, the Ufurper, who being at war with Scotland and Ireland in rebellion, thought fit to deny them equal privileges in commerce. But this loyal Parliament will, I hope, confider that the three kingdoms are not to be thus divided in interefts while under one monarch; and that his naval

Of Trade.

power, their joint ftrength, is increafed by the growth of fhipping in any of them. If the fenfe of this will not prevail to allow them the fame freedoms, yet fure I am they muft from thence perceive England will have a great advantage by fuffering all the king's fubjects of Ireland and Scotland to enjoy the benefit of this act.

There fhould be two free ports appointed, one in the fouth, another in the north, with convenient rules and limitations; and the duty impofed upon any of our exportations, whether of our own growth or manufacture of foreign materials, fhould be not fo high as may either wholly reftrain thofe abroad from buying, or enable others to furnifh them cheaper.

The education of children in foreign parts in colleges or academies fhould be prohibited, and provifion found or made at home for teaching languages and the exercifes of riding, fencing, &c.

Banks and lombards fhould be fpeedily erected, which in a little time would make a

Of Trade.

hundred pounds to be as useful to the public as two hundred real cash is now. But in order thereunto let there be a voluntary registry of land, &c. which in a few years will raise their value considerably. By this way no man indebted, or whose estate is encumbered, is obliged to make discoveries. Yet if he has but half free, the registering of that will the better enable him to discharge the other part. If a registry must not be obtained, at least the selling or mortgaging over and over, secret conveyances, deeds of trust, or any other tricks by which the lender or purchaser is defrauded and abused, should be made felony, without benefit of clergy; and the cheating person obliged to pay the sufferer treble damage, and as much more to the public. This, which certainly all honest men judge as reasonable as what is practised for far smaller evils or offences, will without any innovation in the laws or other alleged inconveniences to the people, secure us to our rights, and, perhaps, answer all the ends of a registry; of which, though very

Of Trade.

convenient, I am not so fond as to think or believe it will so suddenly, or to that height as is said, raise the rents and value of lands. To this it can contribute but by accident, as it invites strangers into the kingdom (for I have already told you that the greater or smaller number of people is the only true cause of the dearness or cheapness of land, and of labour or trade); yet even this it cannot do without abolishing the law disabling aliens to purchase and hold before naturalization; which is necessary without dispute, to be immediately taken away.

Nor would it a little contribute to the general good that all merchants and tradesmen breaking should be made guilty of felony, their goods to the creditors, if they did not plainly make appear by their true books their losses, and discover whatever they have left, and, without the unjust and cunning artifices of composition, give way for an equal dividend among the creditors. And the many abuses of the King's Bench Prison should be reformed, which, as now managed, is

Of Trade.

made a sanctuary and place of refuge and privilege for all knaves that design their own private interest, to the ruin of others, whose confinement is no narrower than from the East to the West Indies.

All bonds and bills obligatory, statute merchants, and of the staple, recognisances, judgments, &c. should be enacted transferable and by indorsement, to pass as current as Bills of Exchange, and made recoverable by a shorter course of law than now practised; that is to say, upon actual proof of the perfecting and last assigning of the deed judgment and execution should be obtained. This would wonderfully enliven trade, make a new species of coin, lower interest, secure in a great measure dealers from breaking, and find money to carry on the trades of fishing, linen, woollen, &c.

Until the proposed regulation of the laws can be effected, to avoid the trouble and charge of juries in many cases, and other unjust vexations, the meets and bounds of the denominations of all lands, manors, parishes,

Of Trade.

commons, hundreds and counties; all prefcriptions, ufages and cuftoms, and the jurifdictions of all inferior courts be fully enquired into and truly regiftered in one book or books; copies to be printed and the original to be, and remain of record, as the Doomfday Book in the Exchequer: by which all difputes concerning the premifes may be fpeedily and cheaply decided.

There are but two objections againft this public good, and were they unanfwerable, yet fince they are but particular and felfifh confiderations they ought not to take place. The firft is, that the ufeful and laudable calling of the lawyers will be prejudiced. The next that the many, who now live upon credit, will be undone. As to the firft, by this work the prefent lawyers will be fo far from fuffering, that for ten years to come, rather than leffen, it will increafe their bufinefs; which, according to the ordinary computation of men's lives or their hopes of being promoted, will be a greater advantage to them than if things continued as they are; and for thofe

Of Trade.

who propose to themselves this way of living there will be still grounds enough for the practice of some, and many new employments for others. So that, if these gentlemen's present great practice would give them leave to look forward, they would find they are more scared than hurt. As to the second sort, who likewise believe they may be damnified, that fancy will also vanish if it be considered that it will enlarge rather than destroy credit. For, we will suppose that a young merchant or tradesman, who has £500 of stock, does not trade for less than £2,000, the merchant that sells him the commodities upon the belief of his being honest, industrious, prudent and sober, gives him credit, and takes his bond payable at a certain day. This person, that he may be able duly to discharge his obligation in like manner, trusts another whom he supposes able and honest; for all receive credit as they really are or appear such. As soon as his bond becomes due, he takes up his own and gives that he received to his creditor, who perhaps, gives it to another to whom he is indebted.

Of Trade.

At laſt the money is called for from the country gentleman; the country gentleman gives him an aſſignment on his tenant, who either is or is not indebted. If the tenant owes the money he pays it in ſpecie, or aſſigns him upon ſome merchant, for the value of commodities ſold him, the fund enabling him to pay his landlord's rent. Thus, perhaps, by a circulation of traffic—for all men from the higheſt to the loweſt are one way or other merchants or traders—the firſt man is paid with his own paper. If the tenant does not owe the landlord the money, and, therefore, will not pay, the landlord is immediately neceſſitated to ſell or mortgage ſome part of his eſtate; which, if he refuſe, the law forces him and the credits of the reſt are ſecured. The conſequences are plainly theſe, that men muſt be careful with whom they deal; that they muſt be punctual and thrifty leſt they firſt loſe their credit, and afterwards become beggars. For, he that rightly conſiders, will be convinced that every man in a ſociety or commonwealth, even

Of Trade.

from the king to the peasant, is a merchant; and, therefore, under a necessity of taking care of his reputation—not seldom a better patrimony than what descends to us from our parent's care. By this practice the kingdom will gain an inexhaustible treasure, and, though there were not a hundredth part of the money, be able to drive ten times a greater trade than now it does. A man thus enabled to live and trade without money, will be in no need of running out his principal in interest, by which too many for want of consideration are insensibly undone, involving many more in their ruin. Without these, or some other new courses, you may be assured that our trade, consequently our power, will every day decay, and in a few years, come to nothing.

But some imagine that we need not trouble ourselves in this matter, it will shortly fall in of course to our country; for that as learning took its circuit through several parts of the world, beginning at the east, so must trade too. But whoever believes this will

Of Trade.

come to pafs without human means, labour and art, entertains wrong notions of Providence.

I do believe the great wheel is always in motion, and though there be a conftant circumgyration of things, yet it is idle to fancy that anything but troubles or wars, oppreffion or injuftice, wit or induftry makes trade or learning fhift their places in the fame country, or alter their abode from that to any other. If we look into hiftories we fhall find thefe have been the caufes of their migration, and that trade and learning ufually go hand in hand together.

Having already afferted that trade and commerce are to be improved and carried on the more vigoroufly by how much the more labour and thrift are increafed; and that the making idlers work is in effect an increafing the people: and that all fuch fhould be forced into feveral workhoufes, (which, though the Parliament has taken into confideration, yet, for want of ftock, is not hitherto put in any forwardnefs,) I will now give you my thoughts

Of Trade.

how this may probably be brought about, with little or no charge but to such only as upon prospect of advantage do change the scenes of their lives, as by marriage, employments, callings, &c. or by assuming new titles and degrees of honour; and consequently as their respective proportions or payments are here proposed, they cannot account them burdensome or grievous. To perfect this, I think it necessary that all hospitals, alms-houses and lands for charitable uses, be sold, and more stately and convenient ones erected, into which none but diseased persons, or others perfectly unable to earn their living, should be received. And to the end they might the sooner be restored to health, a convenient number of physicians, nurses and tenders ought to be appointed, and sufficient salaries established. England, to her great shame, is in this instance much behind her neighbours of France and Holland; in the practice of which I know not whether there be more of charity or of policy, of heavenly or of earthly interest.

Of Trade.

The several directions of the act for raising a stock should be strictly put in execution. All fines for swearing, drunkenness, breaches of the peace, felons' goods, deodands, &c. should for a certain number of years be converted to this use; which would bring in twenty times more than is now received on these accounts, and may perhaps prevent the late much practised trick of finding all *felo's-de-se* mad. All contributions for maintenance of the poor (which are so considerable that I have been told, that in some single parishes in London they amount, *communibus annis*, to five thousand pounds a year) should be added to this stock. And it should be further enacted that every man at his admission to freedom pay one shilling; upon marriage, what he thinks fit above one shilling; every clergyman at ordination ten shillings, at instalment into any dignity, twenty shillings; arch-deacons, three pounds; deans, five pounds; bishops, ten pounds; archbishops, twenty pounds; gentlemen upon admittance into the Inns of Court, ten shillings; upon their being called

Of Trade.

to the bar, forty shillings; when made serjeants, or king's counsel, five pounds. Every man upon admission into the inns of chancery, three shillings and four pence; when sworn attorney, ten shillings; lord high chancellor, keeper, lord high treasurer, and lord privy seal, twenty pounds; chief justice, chief baron, chancellor of the exchequer, master of the rolls, and attorney-general, twelve pounds a-piece; every of the other judges and barons, the solicitor-general and the six clerks, ten pounds a-piece; the masters of chancery and other officers not named in that or other courts, any sum not exceeding six pounds a man, as shall be thought convenient by the respective judges; all knights, five pounds; baronets, ten pounds; barons, viscounts, earls, twenty pounds; dukes and marquesses, fifty pounds; all aldermen of London, twenty pounds; of other cities and corporations, three pounds; mayors, ten pounds; all masters of arts in universities, twenty shillings; doctors of law and physic, forty shillings; of divinity, four pounds; heads and masters of colleges, five pounds; all executors and adminiftrators that undertake the charge, two fhillings; all perfons entering into eftates either by defcent or purchafe, one fhilling, over and above one fhilling for every hundred pounds per annum of fuch eftate. Every Sunday there fhould be collections in all churches of the kingdom, which, with what fhall be received at the Communion, are to be thus appropriated. And all ftreet, door, and other charitable doles in broken meat or money, as the great encouragements and chief occafions of idlenefs and vice, fhould be forbid under fevere penalties. Briefs fhould be iffued through the kingdom for voluntary contributions. The names of fuch as fhall be eminently bountiful fhould be conveyed to pofterity by placing their coats of arms, and regiftering their munificence in the refpective workhoufes of the city, corporation or county where they live. I do not doubt but in a very fhort time a ftock would be thus raifed fufficient to employ all the idle hands in England. And though I believe that after a little while there would be

Of Trade.

no need of ufing art or feverity in bringing people into thefe nurferies of labour and induftry, the fweets of gain and trouble of idlenefs—which certainly is not the leaft of toils to fuch as have been inured to labour or bufinefs—being of themfelves ftrong allurements; yet, to lay the firft foundation with fuccefs, I conceive it neceffary that both men and women who have no vifible ways of maintenance, criminals of what quality foever, punifhed as before in the Difcourfe of Laws, and the children taken out of the Foundling Hofpital, as foon as able to do any thing, be all fent to thefe workhoufes. The great numbers of people going out of this kingdom, Scotland and Ireland to other parts of Europe fhould be reftrained, and none be fpirited into the Weft Indies or fuffered to go abroad unlefs to trade; fuch as by infirmity or age are abfolutely difabled, among which neither the lame nor the blind are to be reckoned, fhould be maintained and confined within the public hofpitals; every conftable in whofe ward or precinct any beggar is found, fhould forfeit twenty pounds; and the perfon or perfons entertaining or lodging any, five pounds, to the ufe of the workhoufe.

Thofe who are commonly fent to the Houfe of Correction or Bridewell, and thofe found guilty of petty larceny, fhould be fent to the workhoufe; for that indeed whipping, the punifhment intended for their amendment, does but take away the fenfe of fhame and honour, rendering them impudent and incorrigible in their iniquities. But granting its operation fo forcible as to be able to reclaim them, yet certain it is that its beft effect is but to hinder them from doing further mifchief; whereas by this courfe not only that will be avoided, but a confiderable profit redound to the public. To thefe alfo fhould be added all prifoners for criminal matters though acquitted, if by circumftances they appear fufpicious; it being reafonable to conclude fome rogues and vagabonds, though the evidence required by ftrictnefs of law be not ftrong enough to convict them. Hither likewife are all to be fent who for trivial inconfiderable caufes, and fometimes out of

Of Trade.

pure malice, are thrown into prisons and there forced to spend the remainder of their miserable lives; the exorbitant extortion of fees and the merciless rage of their enemies swelling their debts beyond the power or hopes of satisfaction, whereby they become not only useless but a burden to the commonwealth. And because the benefit of clergy was introduced for the advancement of learning in the ruder days of our ancestors, and that there is now no such need, the kingdom being so far from wanting that it is rather overstocked in every faculty with such as make learning a trade; and the intercourse of our affairs almost necessitating all others to read and write, I hold it convenient to take it quite away; not only because useless, but because it is an encouragement to many to transgress the bounds of the law. Then all of what degree or condition soever, men or women, literate or illiterate, convicted of any of the crimes for which clergy is now allowed, should be condemned to the workhouses for seven years, or pay to its use sixty pounds or more, according to their qualities.

Of Trade.

By what I have already said you see I am no friend of pardons, but if any must still be granted, then any not a gentleman obtaining one, should pay twenty pounds, a gentleman forty pounds, an esquire sixty pounds, a knight bachelor eighty pounds, a baronet or other knight one hundred pounds, a lord two hundred pounds, a marquis or duke four hundred pounds. The eldest sons of every of these should pay equal with the fathers. And in case after all this, people should be wanting, Ireland may furnish yearly hundreds or thousands of its children; which will prove not only advantageous for increasing the wealth of England, but also for securing the peace and quiet of that kingdom, by making so many of the natives one and the same people with us, which they will soon be, if taken away so young as that they may forget their father's house and language; and if, after seven, eight, or nine years, when masters of their trade, returned into their own, or suffered to abide in this country.

I will not trouble you with recounting in

Of Trade. 231

particular the many advantages that would soon flow through all the tracts of this land from this source of industry, if thus supplied with money and hands. All trades and useful manufactures of silks, linen, canvass, lace, paper, cordage for ships, iron, tin, &c. may be there set on foot, and carried on to a far greater profit than single men can drive them. In this workhouse should be taught the knowledge of arms, and the arts of war, on all festivals and holidays; and the lusty young fellows sent by turns to sea, for a year or two of the time of this their state apprenticeship. By this means the king would be enabled at any time, without pressing, to draw out of this great seminary a sufficient army, either for land or sea-service.

The ways, methods, and orders for regulating the several workhouses I could fully demonstrate, did I not think it needless at present. It is enough that I here promise to do it at any time when the Great Council shall think fit to take this matter into consideration, or when you please to impose your further commands. But give me leave to say, that laying aside all other reformations of the state, this alone would secure our lives and fortunes from violence and depredation, not only increase our wealth and power beyond what now it is, but make them far exceed whatever any of our neighbours are possessed of; and consequently establish a firm and lasting peace at home, and make us terrible to the nations abroad. This great happiness is the wish of every true Englishman, but can only be effected by the care and wisdom of the King and Parliament; to whom I most passionately recommend and humbly submit it.

I have now at length run through all the parts of my uneasy task, you will say, I doubt not, very slubberingly. To be beforehand with you, I do confess it; I never undertook anything more unwillingly, and therefore have performed it, not only ill, but carelessly, studying nothing so much as to come quickly to an end; which, indeed, was my greatest labour. The fields you commanded me to take a turn in, were so

Of Trade.

spacious, that being once entered, considering how short a while you obliged me to stay, I could not easily find my way out again; which put me to a necessity of running, and the haste not giving me leave to see the rubbs in my way, forced me to stumble. What I have done can serve to no other purpose than for hints to enlarge your better thoughts upon.

Had these papers been worthy, I would have presented them by way of new year's gift; but that was not my fault. Most of what you meet with here, we have often discoursed with our ———. You must not read them to any other; for I am persuaded they would tell you the man was mad. Perhaps I was so for writing, but I am sure I have yet madder thoughts, for I do seriously believe all I have here said is true;—and this to boot, that the world is a great cheat, that an honest man or a good Christian is a greater wonder than any of those strange ones, with which Sir H. B. has often entertained us better. This, you are sure of, I have spoken nothing for interest; I am but a bare stander by, no better, and therefore neither win nor lose, let the game go how it will. But to trifle no more, I am not concerned what any think; I live to myself, not others, and build not my satisfaction upon the empty and uncertain vogue or opinion of men. If I did, I should put into their power to make me unhappy whenever they please.

To conclude, the result of all I have here said is, that England might be the happiest country in the world, if the people would be content to make a right use of their power; that is, to act by the rules of reason, on which their own constitutions are founded: for since they have the power of reforming the old and enacting new laws, in which every man (the poorest that is worth but forty shillings per annum) has his vote, no man can be offended with his own act; but, if he be, the remedy is at hand. So that here, everyone living according to reason, and that making every man a judge, all must

Of Trade.

see, to their great comfort, that the interest of the king and people is really one and the same; that the common good is every single man's; and that whoever disturbs the public, injures himself; which is to the whole the greatest security imaginable, and to every private man a lasting happiness.

The laws are not exact, because the Parliament hearken to the counsel, that, not the lawyers, but their interest dictates; neglecting to follow that advice, which they may have for nothing, *viz.* " Let the counsel of thine own heart stand, for there is no man more faithful unto thee than it; for a man's mind is wont to tell him more than seven watchmen that sit above in a high tower." That is, consult with no man who advises with regard to himself; which is plain from these words, " Every counsellor extolleth counsel; but there is that counselleth for himself; beware therefore of a counsellor, and know before what need he hath, for he will counsel for himself; lest he cast the lot upon thee, and say unto thee, 'Thy way is good,' and afterwards he ſtand on the other ſide to ſee what ſhall befall thee." Whether this be a prophecy of what the lawyers will do, or a bare narration of matter of fact, what they daily practiſe, I leave to every diſcerning man's judgment.

The ſhort of this is to adviſe that in making of new laws or in altering or repealing the old, the members truſt not the gentlemen of the long robe, unleſs they promiſe to join the law and the goſpel; to give their advice without money, or the hopes of gain; and yet if their charity or generoſity ſhould perſuade them to undertake the cauſe thus in *forma pauperis*, that they give ſufficient ſecurity, not to ſtarve it; that is, not to be backward in their giving advice according to conſcience, not intereſt.

When this is done, we are not ſecured, unleſs the Parliament provide that no infringer of the laws be pardoned; that is to ſay, that equal juſtice be diſtributed, making no diſtinction between the perſons of the higheſt and the loweſt, when their crimes have made

Of Trade.

them equal. Which cannot probably be otherwife effected, than by conftituting, as is done in Venice, a new magiftracy of public cenfors, who fhall have infpection into the actions of all the courts of judicature and public offices whatfoever; whofe account fhall by the Parliament be received as authentic, and make the offenders obnoxious to degradations and pecuniary mulcts, to the fatisfaction of the injured, and a farther overplus to the public, unlefs in their judgments the accufed fairly acquit themfelves.

Religion as now managed, is made an art or trade to live by, and to enable the profeffors to abufe the credulous and unwary. If intereft be not removed, and not opinions, but a good life be the character to diftinguifh real Chriftians from thofe who pretend themfelves fuch, we fhall never have peace here nor affurance of happinefs hereafter. In granting liberty of confcience clergymen's advice is not to be hearkened to, unlefs they will refign their livings and difpute only for truth. Toleration is at this time more efpecially for three great reafons abfolutely convenient; firſt, to unite us at home; next, to enable us now and hereafter to reſiſt the power of France (this certainly requires all our ſtrength, which without union we cannot have); the third and great reaſon, to advance our trade.

The French are to be ſtopped in their career. To do ſo it is neceſſary a large and ſufficient revenue for ever (if it be done wiſely) be fixed and ſettled on the crown, on the ſtate; I do not ſay on the perſon of the king, for he is indeed, if rightly conſidered, but God's ſteward, and has ſo great a ſhare in the trouble that it is an unreſolved queſtion, notwithſtanding all his glory and power, whether the roſes of the crown make amends for its thorns, and whether the ſoftneſs of any lining can eaſe the weight of the burden he undergoes; whoſe nights and days are made reſtleſs by the preſſures of that mighty care to which by the ſafety of three kingdoms he is continually ſolicited. If half a loaf (as they ſay) be better than no bread, it is more eligible to part with ſome than to expoſe all to the mercy of an enemy and conqueror, from whom the greatest favour we can expect is to become not a subordinate kingdom, but an enslaved province.

Trade is to be promoted by all possible care and diligence, because by that we must be enabled to pay our taxes, without which we cannot withstand foreign violence. Trade is to be bettered by inviting more people into the kingdom and employing all the idle hands we already have. This is to be effected by proposing advantages and rewards to strangers; fit employments, threats and punishments to natives; by ascertaining all, ease and security in their persons, estates and purchases, by an uninterrupted and speedy course of justice, firmly establishing the three great satisfactory desirables,—liberty, property, and religion.

Salus Populi suprema Lex.

From —— this 4th of
    January, 167$\frac{7}{8}$.

      Sir,

       I am, &c.

FINIS.

APPENDIX.

A.

Proofs of Thomas Sheridan's authorſhip of the Tract of 1677.

" This tract, put forth at a critical moment, without name of author, publiſher, or printer, yet actively circulated, may be ſhown in very few words to be even now of great intrinſic intereſt," and a work of Thomas Sheridan of Cavan.—Editor's *Preface*, xxix.

IN 1680, three years after the date of the tract, it was popularly attributed to him as an offence; and in his defence at the Bar of the Commons he meets that imputation in terms which clearly admit the fact of ſuch authorſhip, but denying culpability.

A gift copy of the tract exiſts, with the autograph of Thomas Sheridan, "from the author" on the title page.

In Walter Harris's edition of Sir James Ware's " Notices of Iriſh Writers," details are given from Thomas Sheridan's ſpeech of 1680, word for word, showing that Harris held him to have written the tract.

With thefe original proofs it is needlefs to accumulate recent judgments to the fame effect, fuch as the Rev. Dr. Bandinel's, in the Catalogue of the Bodleian Library; and that of Watts in the Bibliotheca, art. Thomas Sheridan; but it is not without intereft to obferve, that frequent paffages in the tract itfelf point plainly at him for its author.

B.

Pedigree of the Sheridans of the 17th Century.

Dennis O'Sheridan, *alias* Denny Sheridan, married to Fofter,—" My mother, a gentlewoman of England, of good fortune; a Fofter, who for my father's fake, quitted her country and relations; both famous for honefty, for their loyalty and fuffering."—THOMAS SHERIDAN, *Speech at the Bar of the Houfe of Commons*, 1689; Editor's *Preface*, xxviii.

DENNIS SHERIDAN[1] = ... FOSTER.

WILLIAM, Lord Bifhop of Kilmore, b. 1635; d. 1716.	PATRICK, Lord Bifhop of Cloyne, b. 1638; d. 1684.	THOMAS,[2] b. 1646.
THOMAS, b. 1684; the friend of Dean Swift.		SIR THOMAS, b. 1696; d. in France.

---

[1] The Sheridan of the Bifhop of Meath's letter of 1685 to Mr. Boyle.

[2] The author of the tract of 1677, and of the MS. Hiftory

Appendix. 243

C.

The Ulster Custom illustrated.

"Few books would be more useful than a narrative from the abundant sources extant, of the Londoners' settlement in Ireland, for the last 250 years, with its bearing on the famous somewhat obscure Ulster-right."—Editor's *Preface*, xvii.

In Baron Heath's "History of the Grocers' Company," and in a volume upon the Irish Society, by the Member for Hackney, Mr. Reed, we have opening accounts of that settlement; so that more may be expected, seeing how much the Treasury has done of late in like productions for the City records.

---

of the time preserved in the Royal Library at Windsor. What his own social position was is obvious from his speech at the Bar of the House of Commons in 1680, besides the fact that two of his brothers were bishops of the Irish Protestant church. Of this stock came the learned and eccentric friend of Dean Swift, Dr. Thomas Sheridan, born in 1684. Yet in the important work by the Rev. Hugh Rose, art. T. S. he is stated to have sprung from " parents in humble life in the county Cavan." Surely our biographies call for large corrections, as much as our national history.

This little table is purposely limited to the seventeenth century, leaving a fitting continuation to the time when Thomas Sheridan's " history of his time," with his remarkable official career, may be given.

244 *Appendix.*

D.

Bishop Bedell's printed books and MSS.

" The reasons of Bishop Bedell (in favour of using the Irish language in the Proteſtant Church), led a Convocation in 1634 to order that the miniſter ſhould read the Liturgy in Irish; and the pariſh clerk accompany the miniſter in reading that part of the ſervice."—*The Biſhop of Meath to Mr. Robert Boyle,* 1685. Editor's *Preface,* xxii.

A complete catalogue of Biſhop Bedell's productions in print and known MSS., would fill a large volume if properly deſcribed. Here, it ſuffices to ſuggeſt, with brief reaſons, that diligent ſearch will reveal little underſtood treaſures from him. Early in life, with the aſſiſtance of Sir Adam Newton, tutor to Prince Henry Stuart, he publiſhed a tranſlation of Father Paulo's hiſtorical works; and his correſpondence with Sir Adam was publiſhed in Dublin in the beginning of the laſt century. In 1624 he dedicated to the Prince of Wales, Prince Henry's brother, a valuable volume upon the Roman Catholics. When in Venice for eight years he became a ripe Italian ſcholar; and produced at that time uſeful educational works for the uſe of Italian ſcholars who wiſhed to learn Engliſh. At the time of the Popiſh plot of the 5th of November, he wrote " The Proteſtant

Memorial," a Spenferean poem, of which two copies only are known—one in the Britifh Mufeum—the Grenville collection—the other in the Bodleian. His meafure for the reform of Trinity College, Dublin, of which he was for two years Provoft, is alone enough to obtain high repute for fcholarfhip and judgment. When Bifhop, he promoted the ftudy of the Irifh language with great zeal; and the tranflation of the Old Teftament into Irifh, which he corrected, was printed a hundred years later by Mr. Boyle. His correfpondence was extenfive; and no life of the Bifhop fhould be written again without a vigorous inquiry throughout the United Kingdom, and in Venice, Spain, Germany and France for his letters, ftill preferved in MS. His eulogifts are legion, from Coleridge's fententious declaration that Bedell was inferior to none, however lofty in the grand ecclefiaftical hierarchy,—to the late Irifh Chancellor Napier, whofe lecture to young ftudents in Dublin is a mafterpiece. His earlieft biographer, Clogy, who was a member of his family, tells fimply and well what he had witneffed during many years of excellence. Bifhop Burnet's more elaborate record has all the merits and all the faults of that prelate's vigorous pen. One of the MS. lives by Clogy has been recently publifhed from the Harleian copy by Mr. Wilkins, with great care. A valuable feries of letters on the fubject has appeared in "Notes and Queries," by Mr. Moyer of St. John's College, Cambridge; and the ingenious Mr. Monck Mafon has publifhed a later life from records not before examined. Still there feems to remain for more diligent fearch, the Bifhop's correfpondence with the moft eminent fcholars of his time, not only in Ireland and Great Britain, but in Italy, Germany and France. So long ago as by his own will, he gave a MS. Hebrew Bible to his College, Emmanuel, Cambridge.

E.

The Stuart Papers, at Home and Abroad.

" The *Stuart Papers*, from the royal captive in Windfor ' Caftle to the royal exile at St. Germain—from Mary Queen of Scots to the fallen Pretender of '45—of whom the whole truth is not yet told."—Editor's *Preface*, xxxvii.

When Mr. Fox, with the magnanimity belonging to the great popular ftatefman, fought eagerly for the beft evidence favourable to King James II, whofe fall he was to record with honeft fatisfaction, it is to be regretted that the political confufions of the time narrowed that eager refearch fo much.

Appendix. 247

It is certain that with the like difpofition now to examine traces of *all Stuart papers*, far more voluminous collections of them may be difcovered than thofe of which Mr. Fox's agents loft the traces at their fuppofed deftruction in French Flanders.[1] Already we are beginning to learn how many genuine materials of the ftory of "the Scot Abroad"[2] can be recovered at no great coft. A general fpirit prevails to encourage fuch inquiry. All the continental governments are as bufy at the work as we are; and a wife *interchange of the refults* may be hoped for. For example, as to *Stuart Papers* in the public library at Boulogne-fur-mer, there is *catalogued* a valuable MS. of the year 1739,—a letter of 400 folios by Sir Alexander Murray of Stanhope to John, the Duke of Argyle, full of various topics of lafting intereft,—but in particular with a moft remarkable vindication of King James II. in regard to the Duke of Monmouth. If Lord Macaulay had read this MS. in his dozen vifits to Boulogne, his harfh view of that incident muft have foftened. So for another time in the north of France there are fome melancholy

---

[1] Lord Holland's Preface to Mr. Fox's *Fragments*.
[2] The title of Mr. Burton's Scottifh Emigrants' book.

footsteps of exiles, who were present at the execution of the Queen of Scots, in the case of one of her ladies; and of another whose descendants live honoured among us. Again at Arras, the memory of Sir Thomas More is enshrined. In the Vatican again, what Stuart treasures there are, of which Bishop Burnet was admitted in his day to see some; Mr. Canning authorised the purchase of others, now in the British Museum. Probably in that venerable repository may be found the Canterbury Registers of five centuries ago, carried off by an unlucky archbishop. So the Pepys papers, at Cambridge, have letters of Charles II.; and the young Pretender's march to and from Derby left traces still to be read in the muniment rooms of such mansions as Bolsover. There is no end of such things, and they are crowned by *Thomas Sheridan's* MS. history of his time, preserved in the royal library at Windsor.

INDEX.

LLEYN, Edward, of Dulwich, xxxix.
Anglo-Saxons, 18.
Anthologia, Hibernica, xi.
Aquinas, lii.
Appendix, 241.
Arians, the firſt diſſenters perſecuted, lvi.

Ballot in Elections, 27.
Banks and lombards to be eſtabliſhed, 214.
Bedell, Biſhop, Dedication to, v.
————— b. 1570, xvii.; d. 1641, xviii.
————— the Apoſtolic Biſhop, xli.
————— his learning, tolerance and public ſpirit, generoſity and popularity with the Iriſh Roman Catholics, xvii. xxxi. and xli.
Bellarmine, lii.
Bills and bonds to be circulated and be payable to bearer, 215-7.
Boyle, the Hon. Robert, xxii.
Britiſh, the, 18.
Burnet, Biſhop, xxv. xxxv.

Bury, Richard of, on Education in 1330, xxxii.
Buxton, Sir Fowell, xl.

Cafaubon, liii.
Cenfors, Public, wanted, 66.
Charity and Church Funds to be realized and collectively adminiftered, 107-223.
Charles I. prophecy on, 40.
Chriftianity, True, li.
Civilization of Ireland in 1290 and 1608, xiv.
Clarendon Correfpondence, the, xxxvi.
Clogy, Rev. Mr., xxv.
Coffee Houfes, 4.
Coin to be exportable, 209.
Companies, privileged, to be put down, 196.
Conqueror, William the, 32.
Conquefts, evil, viii. xii. xiv.
Conftantine the Great, perfecutor, lvi.
Corruption of the time, 2.
County Court of old, 65.
Courts of Judicature, 4.
——————————— to be thoroughly recaft, 57-63.
Croydon, education in, xxxii.
Cuftoms and rates to be remodelled, 169.

Danes, 18.
Davies, Sir John, on Irifh conquefts, xiii.
Death punifhments, all, to be abolifhed, 44-56.
Debates in Parliament, 27.
Diffenters to be tolerated, lx.
Documents, Public, returned from the United States, xiv.

Index.

Druids, 18.
Drummond, Thomas, on Ireland x. xi. xxxix.

Education to be univerſal, xxxi. and xxxiii.
Electors of M.Ps., to be choſen by all hundreders, 25.
——————— their duties, 26.
Ellis, Sir Henry, original letters of, xxxvi.
England weak in 1677, 4.
Equity and law to be combined as of old, 62.
Exciſe, the beſt tax if impoſed equally, 172.

Factions odious, 30.
Fiſheries to be promoted, 193.
Foſter ——, wife of Dennis Sheridan, 1635, xxviii.
France, Louis XIV., ambitious of univerſal conqueſt, 114, 145.
Free ports to be opened, 214.
Friefland, Weſt, conſtitution of, like our own, 19.

Goldſmith, O., xxvi.
Government, Origin of, 8.

Habeas Corpus Act, xxxv.
Harding's Satires on Croydon, xxxiv.
Hearth-money to be aboliſhed, 174.
Hibernica, the, xi.
Hierocles, 81.
Hiſtorian, Public, wanted, 68.
Hiſtorical MSS. Commiſſion, xxxviii.
Hiſtory, 68.
Holland, wife conſtitution of, 14.

Impiety to be ſuppreſſed, lxii.

Index.

Ireland to be ruled in all refpects on an equality with England, 138-144.
Irenæus, li.
Irifh capabilities, x.
—— friendly union with, vii.
Ivery, Houfe of, xi.

James I., liii.
James II., xxxvi.
Judges not to make law, 64.
Juftinian code, lvi.

Kilkenny, Statutes of, 1367, xv.

Languages to be learned, xli.
Laws, 4-34.
—— Code of, wanted, 35.
———— intended by the Long Parliament, but ftopped by Cromwell, 38.
—— Common and Statute, 42.
Lawyers diftrufted, 40.
Lucas, Frederick, M.P., xxxix.

Macintofh, Sir James, xxxvi.
Macartney, Lord, xlii.
Macaulay, Lord, xxxvi.
Manichees perfecuted, lviii.
Merit at fchool to be rewarded, xxxiii.
Monarchy, rife of, 10.
Moore, Thomas, on Ireland, xii.

Nations differ in character only through government, not through race or climate, viii.

Index. 253

Navigation Act to be repealed as to Ireland and Scotland, 213.
Newton, Sir Adam, tutor to Prince Henry Stuart, 1607, xxxvii.
Novatian diffenters, liii.

O'Connell, Mr., xxxix. xl.
Ormond, Houfe of, MSS. of, xi.
Owenfon, Mifs, in Ireland, xii.

Parliaments, Rife of, 4-6, 19-21, 25.
———— Debates in, 27.
———— to be preferved pure, 31.
Patentees to be rewarded, not privileged, 191.
Paterfon, founder of the Bank of England, xxxix.
Perron, Cardinal, liii.
Perfecution, the firft religious, lvii.
Philips, Sir T., 1630, xvi.
Poll tax, good, if fairly diftributed, 176.
Poor to be employed, xxxi. xxxiv. and 227.
Population to be enlarged, 183-190.
Property, 4.
———— duties of, ix.
Protection againft writs to be abolifhed, 206.
Public men's duty, 3.
Punifhments, 17.

Records, 7.
Religion, 4, 74.
Religious toleration, 75, 88, and 94.
Revenues, 12.
Riches, public, land and labour the fource of, 182.
Rofe, The Rev. H., xxv.

St. Auguftine tolerant, lviii.
— Chryfoftom, lv.
— Hilary, lii.
Salvian tolerant, lix.
Schools for all, and merit to be advanced, 97 and 108.
——— no whipping in, 105.
——— teaching in, to be governed by popular election, 107.
Sheridans of the 17th century, xxiv. and Appendix C.
——— Dennis, xxiii. xxiv. xxv. and xxvii.
——— Thomas, his tract of 1677, x. xxvii. xxviii. and xxxv.
Smith, Adam, xxxix.
Stanton, young, at Pekin, xlii.
Statutes cited, 24 Geo. III. 1784, and 33 Geo. III. 1793, viii.
Stuart Papers, xxxvii. and Appendix E.
——— Prince Henry, xxxvii.
Sumptuary laws wanted, 207.
Sword-men of Ulfter banifhed, xiii.

Taxes, 4, 146-80.
Tertullian, li and liv.
Theodofius tolerant, liii.
——————— in Code, lvi.
Toleration a duty, l.
Tract of 1677, xxix.
Trade, 4.
——— imports not to exceed exports, 183.
——— retail, women only to be employed in, 192, and 229.
——— a great council of, wanted, 182.

Ulfter fettlements of 1609, xiii. xvi.
——— cuftom and right, xvii.
Unity among Chriftians a duty, xxxi.

Index.

Venice, wife conftitution of, 13.

Ware, Sir James, on Irifh writers, xxvii.
Weights and meafures to be reformed, 205.
Wellefley, Col. Arthur, in Ireland, xi.
Woollen manufactures to be encouraged, 194, 199.
Whitgift's, Archbifhop, fchool in Croydon, xxxiii.
Windfor, Royal Library at, xxxvi.

WORKS BY THE EDITOR.

"Multa,—fortaffe multum."

On Schools.

PETITION IN CHANCERY TO REVIVE THE DECAYED GRAMMAR SCHOOL AT STEYNING, SUSSEX, 1816. The fuit fucceeded.
LETTER ON DECAYED GRAMMAR SCHOOLS. In the Gentleman's Magazine, Dec. 1816.
EVIDENCE BEFORE THE CHARITY COMMISSIONERS ON THAT SCHOOL, 1819.
LETTER TO MR. BROUGHAM ON ENDOWED GRAMMAR SCHOOLS, 1819.
TRACT ON THE SAME SUBJECT. Pamphleteer. 1820.
TRACT ON INFANT SCHOOLS. Cape Town. 1824.
PAPERS ON GRAMMAR SCHOOLS. Ecleétic Review.
DULWICH GRAMMAR SCHOOL. Third Edition. 1854.
PAPER ON FISHING-NET BRAIDING SCHOOLS, introduced from Boulogne, 1868.

Law and Adminiftration.

TRACT AS TO LEGITIMATE LIMITS OF MILITARY OBEDIENCE. Pamphleteer. 1822.
SIR ORLANDO BRIDGEMAN'S JUDGMENTS IN THE COMMON PLEAS IN 1660—7; fhowing praétically the great value of our MS. law learning. 1823.

Works by the Editor.

THE LAW ADMINISTRATION OF NEW SOUTH WALES from 1787 to 1826; mainly in 1824-5-6; shewing the evil of convict colonies, and of severe punishments. 1828.
THE LAWS AND CONSTITUTIONS OF THE UNITED STATES. 1830.
OFFICIAL MORALS. Westminster Review, Oct. 1832.
TRACT ON THE RIGHT TO BE HEARD IN ROYAL REFERENCES TO THE PRIVY COUNCIL. 1839.
TRACT ON THE ABOLITION OF TRANSPORTATION, AND ON THE REFORM OF THE COLONIAL OFFICE. 1839.
SPURS TO ADMINISTRATIVE REFORMERS. 1854.

History, and Philanthropy in the Colonies, India, and China.

HUMANE POLICY IN THE COLONIES; shewing the uses of free, just, and integral union of coloured people with us, by the example of South Africa; and according to a measure framed for Canada in 1823 at the instance of the Secretary of State. 1830.
BRITISH COLONIZATION AND COLOURED TRIBES; shewing the same from all our history. 1837.
TRACTS AND OFFICIAL PAPER FOR A COLONY AT NATAL. 1830, &c.
PAPERS FOR THE ABORIGINES PROTECTION SOCIETY. 1836-7.
THE HEREFORD MAP OF A.D. 1270, with a fac-simile of its British Isles. 1849.
LETTER TO SIR C. L. EASTLAKE ON MAPS OF A LARGE UNIFORM SCALE FOR THE NEW HOUSES OF PARLIAMENT. 1849. Third Edition.

Works by the Editor.

PLAN OF A CABOT LIBRARY OF VOYAGES AND COLONIAL ENTERPRISE. 1849.

THE CLASSICAL SOURCES OF OUR HISTORY; shewing the fatal evil of conquests from the example of the Cæsars; and demonstrating the ancient existence of philanthropy. 1849.

THE LIFE AND TRIALS OF PATERSON OF DUMFRIES, founder of the Bank of England. 1859.

THE WRITINGS OF PATERSON, Second Edition, 3 Vols. 1862.

THE LAST DESIGNS OF WILLIAM III. 1860.

THE UNIONS OF 1706, A MODEL FOR ALL UNIONS. 1860.

CORRESPONDENCE WITH THE ITALIAN MINISTERS ON IMPROVING THEIR 8,000,000 SHEEP. 1864.

A PETITION TO THE HOUSE OF COMMONS, in 1869, upon the Free, Just, and Integral Union of Coloured People and us, with digests of material intelligence from beyond sea as used from 1696 to 1709.

THE FIRST FRENCH VOYAGE TO CHINA IN 1688, a translation of the MS. Journal; shewing the Chinese Rulers and People to be willing to receive Foreigners on reasonable terms. 1862.

REVELATIONS OF IRISH HISTORY, AND SHERIDAN'S TRACT OF 1677, ON " LIBERTY, RELIGION, AND TRADE. This is the work here published.

REVIEWS AND MAGAZINES, 1816 to 1867.—The Gentleman's Magazine, Retrospective Review, New Monthly Magazine, The Jurist, The Westminster, Eclectic, Foreign Quarterly, Social Science Review, The Athenæum, Builder, &c. French Reviews from 1833 to 1836—all on Schools, " Official Morals," Colonies, Law, Biography, &c. &c.

NEWSPAPERS from 1808 to 1869, on Schools, Local History, Juvenile Reformation, Employment at home for Discharged Prisoners, Biography, &c.

Works by the Editor.

Biographical Notices.

Denis Papin of Blois; Claude Fauriel; Herder as a vindicator of the lefs civilifed nations; Count von Bifmarck at Biarritz, and Jules Cefar by the Emperor of the French; Thomas Pringle; Edward Rufhton the elder, of Liverpool; Sarah Martin, of Yarmouth; the elder Brant, the Mohawk Chief; Dr. Vanderkemp; Paterfon, of Dumfries; John William Bannifter, R.N., and Chief Juftice of Sierra Leone; Dr. Bedell, of Effex, Bifhop of Kilmore; J. J. Gurney; and William Penn upon Hiftory.

John Robinfon, of Sleafby, in Yorkfhire; peafant born, Grammar fchool taught, Fellow of Oriel, Envoy in Sweden 20 years, the laft Prelate who was a Member of the Cabinet, Lord Privy Seal, Diplomatift, an eminent Patron of Merit, and the originator of the two Profefforfhips of Modern Hiftory in Oxford and Cambridge. MS.

Prepared Works.

LOCAL HISTORY.—(1852.) THE GUILD ROLLS OF PRESTON, in Lancafhire, from the early Plantagenets to the laft Guild, with Notices of Eminent Members and of Family Viciffitudes.

(1868.) PLAN OF A BIOGRAPHICAL RECORD OF CROYDON, from the author of "Philobiblon," Richard of Bury, a Rector of Croydon, and Chancellor to King Edward III., down to Archbifhop Whitgift, and to the Eminent Mafters of his Grace's reviving Grammar School—John Oldham, "the Englifh Juvenal," and Milles, the author of the "Spirit of Generofity," in the "Foundation of Charities."

DOVER IN ITS RELATIONS WITH THE MORINI AND OTHER BELGIANS IN ANTE-ROMAN AGES.

Works by the Editor.

The value of Local Hiſtory was well declared by Dr. Ducarel, the annaliſt of Croydon, in the laſt century, in theſe words:— " I deſpair of a complete hiſtory of this kingdom being written until local antiquities become the taſte of the age"—an anticipation which much is being done to realize.

THE POEMS OF OCLAND, the firſt Head-Maſter of St. Olave's Grammar School, Southwark. A volume upon Engliſh Hiſtory, ſent by order of Queen Elizabeth to all our Grammar Schools.

N.B. Theſe titles of books long prepared by the Editor, are here given in the hope that in more capable hands they may be publiſhed worthily of their intrinſic value.

AN OCTOGENARIAN'S LEGACY TO HIS GRANDCHILDREN, or Chapter III. in his Life's Story. MS. 1870.

MY RELATIONS WITH LIBRARIES, AND SOME OF THEIR KEEPERS. —(1802) The Lewes Library Society and Little Adams. (1807) Penſhurſt, Knoll, and Tunbridge Wells Library. (1809) Queen's College, Oxford. (1812) Nottingham and Lichfield. (1842 to 1870) Britiſh Muſeum. (1818) Buckingham Palace Library and Nicholas Carliſle. (1818) Stowe. (1819) Ruſſell Inſtitution and Lincoln's Inn. (1820) The Tower Records and Mr. Petrie. (1823) Rouen and Paris. (1823) The Board of Trade and George Chalmers. (1824) Cape Town, in South Africa. (1825) Miſſionary Library in Otaheite. (1827) Canton. (1828) Bethelſdorp and Dr. Vanderkemp's MSS. (1830) The Bodleian and the Rev. Dr. Bandinel. (1833) Heidelberg and Bonn. (1834) Paris. (1835) Treves and Frankfort. (1840) Middle Temple and Inner Temple. (1841) The London Inſtitution and Zion College. (1844)

Works by the Editor.

The City Library, Guildhall. (1849) The State Paper Office. (1850) The Advocates' Library; Edinburgh, Manchefter and Liverpool Libraries. (1852) Decayed Libraries in Hereford, Henley-on-Thames, Guildford, and Lewes. (1853) Cambridge Public Library. (1855) Dumfries. (1867) Arras and Boulogne Public Libraries. (1868) The Pavilion Library, Brighton. (1870) The Public Record Office. (1840) The Colonial Society and its Special Collections; its Founders and their Objects; its Break up. (1849) The Library of the Royal College of Phyficians; its MSS. (1850) The Lambeth Archiepifcopal Library. (1850) The Royal Geographical Society and its Library; Admiral Smythe. (1850) The Royal Society's Archives; its early Secretary, Papin, and Mons. De la Sauffaye of Blois. (1820—70) Old Book Stalls and Shops. (1826) My own Library ruined in New South Wales.

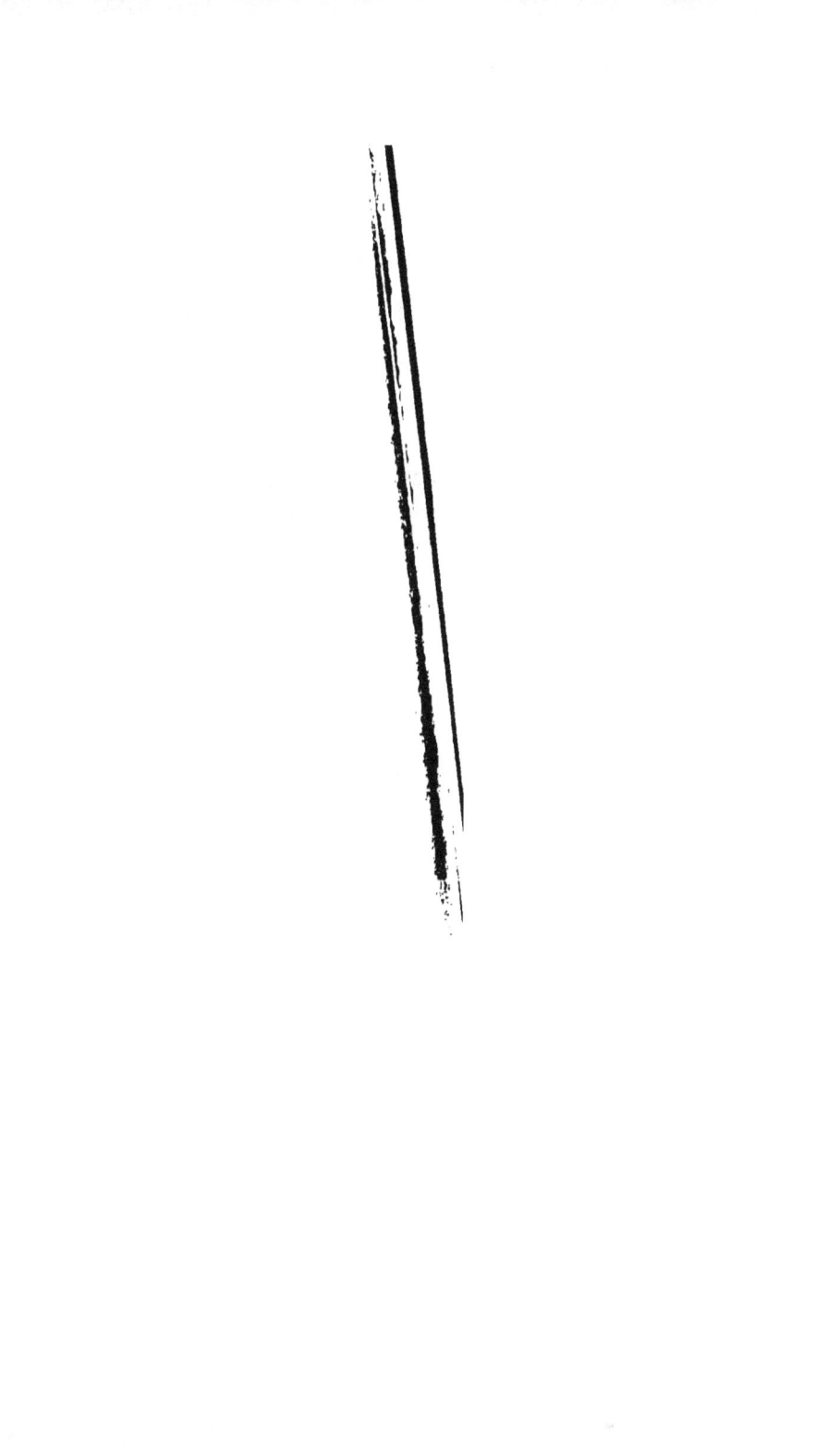

PLEASE DO NOT REMOVE
CARDS OR SLIPS FROM THIS POCKE

UNIVERSITY OF TORONTO LIBRARY

DA   Sheridan, Thomas
957   Some revelations in I
S45   history
1870

www.ingramcontent.com/pod-product-compliance
Lightning Source LLC
Chambersburg PA
CBHW031853220426
43663CB00006B/603